LAND USE HISTORY FOR CEDAR CREEK AND BELLE GROVE NATIONAL HISTORICAL PARK

INTRODUCTION

PRE-HISTORY TO THE BATTLE OF CEDAR CREEK

POST WAR TO THE GREAT DEPRESSION

GREAT DEPRESSION TO THE PRESENT

By Michael Commisso
Historical Landscape Architect
With H. Eliot Foulds, Project Manager
Historical Landscape Architect

National Park Service, Boston, Massachusetts, August 2007

The Olmsted Center for Landscape Preservation promotes the stewardship of significant landscapes through research, planning and sustainable preservation maintenance. The Center accomplishes its mission in collaboration with a network of partners including national parks, universities, government agencies and private nonprofit organizations. Techniques and principles of preservation practice are made available through training and publications. The Olmsted Center perpetuates the tradition of the Olmsted firms and Frederick Law Olmsted's lifelong commitment to people, parks and public spaces.

Olmsted Center for Landscape Preservation
Boston National Historical Park
Charlestown Navy Yard, Quarters C
Boston, MA 02129
www.nps.gov/oclp/

Cover Photo: Photograph of Solomon Heater Farmstead. Source: OCLP, 2006.

TABLE OF CONTENTS

LIST OF FIGURES, TABLES AND DRAWINGS

LIST OF FIGURES

LIST OF TABLES

LIST OF DRAWINGS

Land Use History for Cedar Creek and Belle Grove National Historical Park

ACKNOWLEDGMENTS

The Olmsted Center would like to thank Community Planner, Christopher Stubbs and Superintendent, Diann Jacox, staff at Cedar Creek and Belle Grove National Historical Park for their assistance and contributions to this report.

Special thanks go to Roland Duhaime and colleagues at the University of Rhode Island, for their advice and invaluable technical assistance in the development of georeferenced aerial images and historic maps. Thanks are also due to Clarence Geier and Kim Tinkham with James Madison University and Michael Clarke, planner with Wallace, Roberts and Todd, LLC, for providing research information and guidance throughout the project.

We also appreciate the staff members of the repositories who were helpful and informative in providing research assistance. These include, Handley Regional Library, Warren County Heritage Society and Carrier Library at James Madison University.

INTRODUCTION

PURPOSE OF THIS REPORT

This report provides a brief land use history of the Cedar Creek and Belle Grove National Historical Park and is intended to inform the development of the park's General Management Plan. This report will assist in developing long-range plans by providing an understanding of landscape significance and integrity, identifying areas within the park landscape that reveal its history and where historical interpretations would be most effective. In particular, the report documents change in the pattern of field and forest, views and vistas, roads and transportation corridors and settlement. The presentation of the land use history is organized into time periods pertaining to critical events and milestones and is illustrated with maps and photographs.

PROJECT SETTING

Located within the Shenandoah Valley, the Cedar Creek and Belle Grove National Historical Park is nationally significant as a Civil War battlefield landscape and antebellum plantation. It illustrates the history of the Shenandoah Valley from early settlement through the Civil War and beyond and the battle of Cedar Creek and its significance in the conduct of the war in the Shenandoah Valley.

Created in 2002, the National Park boundary includes publicly and privately owned land and encompasses approximately 3,500 acres within three counties in the northern portion of Virginia (Drawing 0.1). With only eight acres owned by the National Park Service, various partners including Belle Grove Inc., Cedar Creek Battlefield Foundation, Shenandoah Valley Battlefields Foundation, Shenandoah County and the National Trust for Historic Preservation, collectively own 1179 acres and protect another 32 acres with conservation easements.

SHENANDOAH VALLEY REGION

Located within the Valley and Ridge physiographic province, the Shenandoah Valley is bounded by the Blue Ridge to the east, the Appalachian and Allegheny Plateaus to the west, the Potomac River on the north and the City of Roanoke to the south (Figure 0.1). Generally, sandstones compose the ridge tops and carbonate rocks, such as limestone, form the valleys.[1] The soils found within the Valley are considered fertile and productive for agricultural purposes, being weathered from parent limestone, dolomites, sandstones, siltstones and acidic shales.

A distance of 140 miles, the Shenandoah Valley encompasses two counties in West Virginia: Berkeley and Jefferson; and seven counties in Virginia; Frederick, Clark, Warren, Shenandoah, Page, Rockingham and Augusta. Berkeley, Jefferson, Frederick, Clarke and Warren Counties are referred to as the Lower Valley, while the counties south of Strasburg are known as the Upper Valley.

Topography varies within the Valley, consisting of a series of narrow, elongated, forested knobs and ridges created by geological forces over five hundred million years ago. A unique feature to the Valley is Massanutten Mountain, a complex ridge that extends for roughly fifty miles through the center of the Valley, separating it into two smaller valleys. The Shenandoah River is the major water source. As a tributary of the Potomac, the Shenandoah and its tributaries drain several lateral valleys on the west slope of the Blue Ridge. Flowing in a northerly direction, the river is divided by the Massanutten Mountain into the North and South Forks. The two branches join just north of Front Royal, flowing northward to its confluence with the Potomac at Harpers Ferry.[2]

SCOPE OF WORK AND METHODOLOGY

In order to provide the General Management Plan team with timely information related to the cultural landscape, this report relies extensively on secondary sources. The report does not provide an in-depth site history, as is typically found in a Cultural Landscape Report. It instead provides an overview of the landscape's history illustrated with period plans, documenting the landscape's evolution and general character.

Through a concise chronological narrative, the following report documents the history of the landscape and its most significant landscape characteristics. It is organized into three sections corresponding to distinct periods in the development of the park landscape. The periods are Pre-History to the Battle of Cedar Creek, Post War to the Great Depression and Great Depression to the Present.

Beginning with a brief overview of the park's historical context, each section is divided into two subsections. The first subsection, Shenandoah Valley Landscape Features, describes landscape characteristics and features prevalent in the Shenandoah Valley region during each period. Landscape characteristics and features include land use, circulation, buildings and settlement patterns and views and vistas. Through an analysis of landscape characteristics and features, the second subsection, Summary Description of the Study Area, documents the character of the landscape within the boundary of the park.

For the purpose of this report, the term "study area" will refer to the area contained within the legislated boundary of the park.

NATIONAL REGISTER SIGNIFICANCE

Cedar Creek Battlefield and Belle Grove was designated a National Historical Landmark on August 11, 1969, encompassing 900 acres. Cedar Creek Battlefield is significant as the site of the last decisive conflict in the Shenandoah Valley during the Civil War. Belle Grove Plantation, one of the first manor houses built in the Valley, served as the headquarters of Union General Philip Sheridan. The period of significance extends from 1797, the year Belle Grove was constructed, to 1864 the year of the Battle of Cedar Creek. In addition to the property's National Historic Landmark designation, Belle Grove, individually listed in the National Register in 1973, derives significance in the areas of architecture and history. The National Register Information System Database also indicates additional significance for association with James Madison.

A special resource study was prepared in response to the requirements of the Shenandoah Valley Battlefields National Historic District and Commission Act of 1996 (P.L. 104-333). The study area encompassed 22,000 acres. The legislation required the National Park Service to determine whether the District or components thereof met the criteria for designation as a unit of the National Park System. As a result of this special resource study, Cedar Creek and Belle Grove National Historical Park was authorized on December 19th, 2002. The park is located within the Shenandoah Valley Battlefields National Historical District and is managed by the National Park Service, in partnership with several non-profit and municipal entities.

Cedar Creek and Belle Grove National Historical Park commemorates the nationally significant Civil War landscape and Belle Grove Plantation. In addition to its military significance, previously established by the National Historic Landmark designation, the park includes well preserved cultural and natural features from early settlements and examples of the historic agricultural practices and its associated community that once defined the northern Shenandoah Valley.[3]

The existing National Register of Historic Places documentation recognizes military and architectural significance. Additional potential areas of significance include early settlement, agricultural practices, archeology, and ethnography. Further significance may include James Madison's association with Belle Grove and early settler Jost Hite's role in the development of the area.

SUMMARY OF FINDINGS

Since the eighteenth century until the mid-twentieth century when the Interstate Highway System was superimposed upon the Shenandoah Valley, the rural and agricultural character of the landscape was a tangible product of early settlement within the Valley. These landscape patterns were organized according to the availability of natural resources such as fertile soils, water for drinking and powering mills and local industries. Patterns of field and forest were especially durable. During this period of time, the largest portions of woodland occupied the steep topography to the south and east of the study area, with tillage and grazing lands found on the more gentle ground to the north. Landowners sited buildings and structures in clusters supporting individual farms, or within the well-defined boundaries of small towns and villages. For much of the centuries-long period, movement between farms and villages was organized by the Valley Pike, later known as U.S. 11. This central artery has long served as the main route through the study area, with secondary local roads branching from it. Greatly shaped by the natural systems and topography, the historic landscape character remained rural and agricultural, where most residents lived as well as worked until after World War II.

With the exception of landscape changes brought on by the construction of Interstate 81 (I-81), Interstate 66 (I-66) and more recent residential, industrial and commercial developments, Cedar Creek and Belle Grove National Historical Park overall retains a high level integrity. Within the study area, many eighteenth and nineteenth century natural and cultural resources remain intact, especially in the area of the park south and east of I-81. Its rural character remains preserved and the topography and landscape patterns that evoke early settlement and the Civil War are present to help visitors understand the physical development of the Valley region, as well as the strategic role of the landscape in the unfolding of the historic battle.

While extensive highway development in the early 1970s and more recent residential development have altered topographic features, such as Hupp's Hill, the majority of natural and human manipulated topography associated with the park's significance has remained undisturbed. These features which include, Pout's Hill, Three Top Mountain (Signal Knob), Stickley Hill, Thoburn's Run, Stony Hill and the XIX and VIII (Thoburn's) earthworks, were not only significant to the military outcome of the Battle at Cedar Creek, but they also influenced early settlement patterns.

As a result of natural and cultural factors, the mosaic of wooded and open land has regularly shifted within the Shenandoah Valley and the study area. However, despite shifting land uses, the majority of the southern portion of the study area has remained forested throughout its documented history, while the northern portion has remained relatively open. As shown in Table 0.1, with the exception of orchards, the various land uses within the park have remained relatively consistent since the mid-nineteenth century. The column, "Other," includes cemeteries, circulation and buildings. Although topography contributes to the location of settlements, the large number residential and commercial buildings west of I-81 may be attributed to the vast amounts of open land.

LANDUSE SUMMARY AT CEDAR CREEK AND BELLE GROVE NHP				
	Forest	**Field/Agricultural**	**Orchard**	**Other**
1864	38%	58%	3%	1%
1937	36%	50%	13%	1%
2002	40%	55%	2%	3%

Table 0.1: Land Use Summary at Cedar Creek and Belle Grove National Historical Park. Percentages were abstracted from Drawings 1.0-1.2 using GIS software. Source: OCLP 2007.

Overall, most roads and buildings found within the study area in the eighteenth and nineteenth centuries are present today. In areas where roads have been abandoned, historic traces remain. However, additional corridors and buildings have been introduced to the area within the last 60 years. Roads have branched out from the Valley Turnpike (U.S. 11) and I-81 has divided the area in half. While there are some scatterings of new buildings within the park boundaries, the majority of residential, commercial, and industrial development is occurring outside the park boundary near the Town of Strasburg, Middletown and the I-81 and U.S. 11 interchange. With the increase in development within and adjoining the study area, the historic character of the landscape is rapidly changing.

Besides development pressures, mining has greatly increased in recent years. Quarrying may have been important to settlement and development during the historic period, but the increased activity at an industrial scale along the northern portion of the study area has the potential to destroy resources significant to the park, as well as historic views.

While many of the features contributing to the character and significance of the study area remain intact, threats to the rural character of the landscape are foreseeable. According to the Shenandoah, Warren and Frederick counties zoning maps, the majority of the land within the boundaries of the study area is zoned for conservation or agriculture. However, there are many areas outside the boundaries that are zoned for industrial, commercial and residential uses. Zoning for agriculture and conservation within the study area will encourage the perpetuation of rural landscape character, but the areas zoned industrial, commercial and residential beyond the park's boundary will negatively impact viewsheds and ultimately lead to the widening of rural roads in order to increase their capacity.

I-81 and I-66 play a significant role in linking the Shenandoah Valley with the Washington Metropolitan area. In order to serve the growing traffic volumes, the Virginia Department of Transportation has determined that I-81 will require expansion. As a result of the pending highway widening, over 200 residential structures and commercial businesses may be displaced in Shenandoah and Warren counties.[4]

To mitigate additional impacts to the study area, park partners will need to work collaboratively and creatively with private land owners and the Virginia Department of Transportation to preserve and protect natural and historic resources.

Additional opportunities for collaborative landscape preservation exist throughout the park area, however preservation opportunities are especially rich east of I- 81. Here isolated between the highway and the Shenandoah River, the landscape retains a great deal of integrity. Preservation efforts have initially begun in the southern portion of the study area with the acquisition of conservation easements by various partners.

ENDNOTES FOR LAND USE HISTORY INTRODUCTION

[1] Charles B. Hunt, *Natural Regions of the United States and Canada* (San Francisco (CA: W.H.Freeman and Company, 1967) 260.

[2] William G. Thomas III, "The Chesapeake Bay," *Southern Spaces,* April 16, 2004, http://southernspaces.org/contents/2004/thomas/2b.htm.

[3] Congress, House, *Cedar Creek and Belle Grove National Historical Park Act,* 107[Th] Cong., *Public Law 107-373* (Dec. 19, 2002): 16 USC 410iii.

[4] Clarence R. Geier, et al. A*n Overview and Assessment of Archaeological Resources and Landscapes within Lands Managed by Cedar Creek and Belle Grove National Historical Park: Volume One* (Harrisonburg, VA: Department of Sociology and Anthropology, James Madison University, 2006) 179-186.

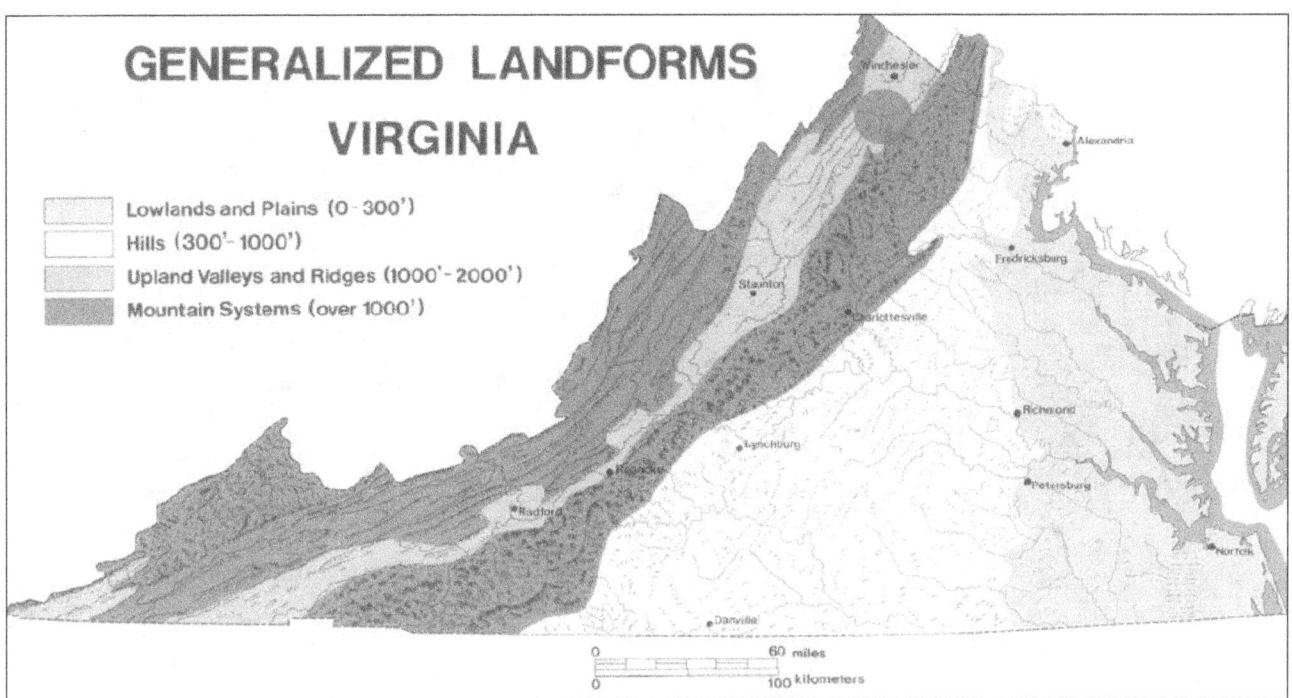

Figure 0.1: A map identifying the geography of the State of Virginia. The Shenandoah Valley is contained within the upland valley and ridge systems. Source: Kuennecke, Bernd, *An Atlas of Virginia: 17th, 18th, and Early 19th Centuries.* (Dubuque, Iowa: Kendall/Hunt, 1989)

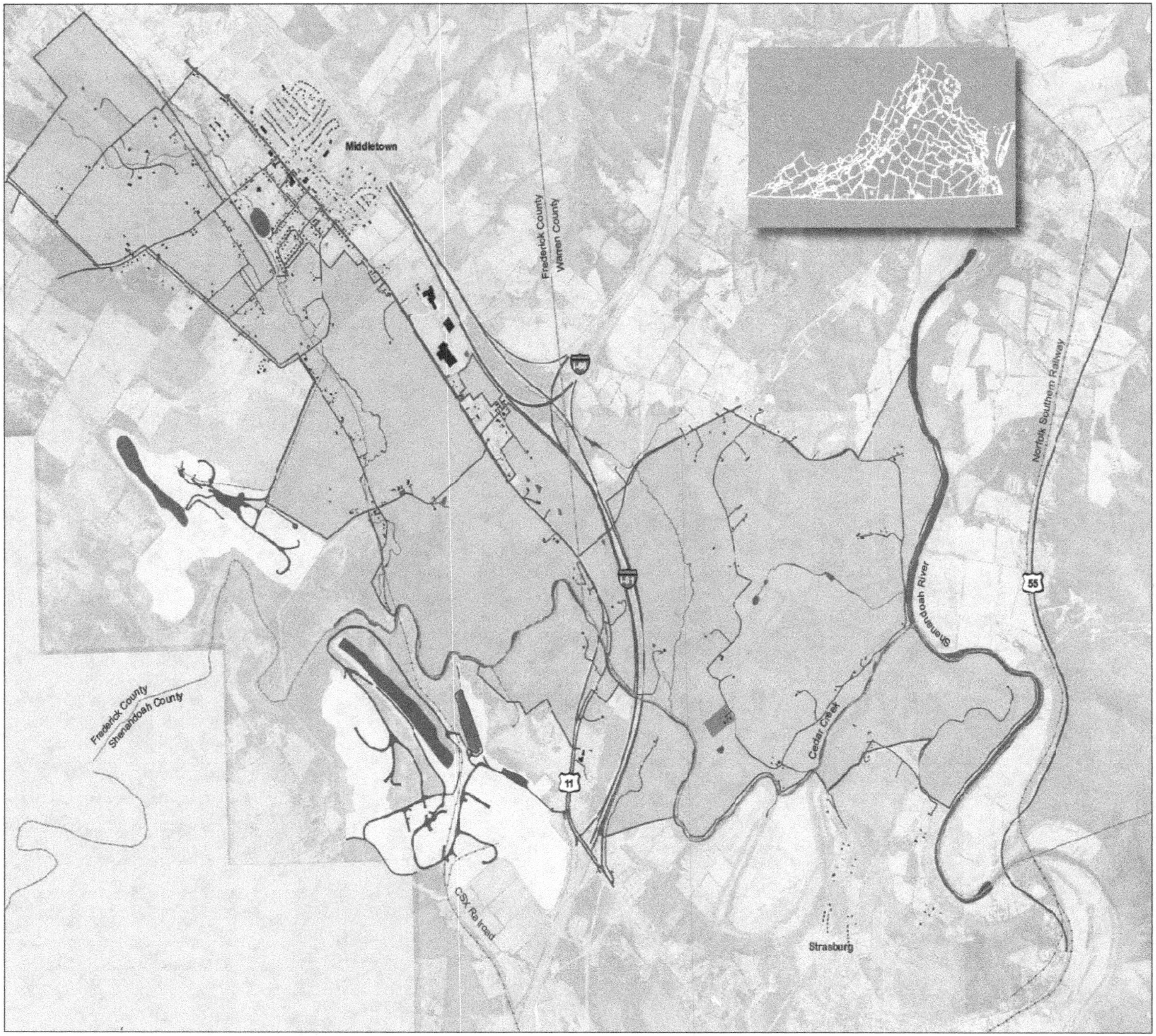

Land Use History Plan

Cedar Creek and Belle Grove National Historical Park

Frederick, Warren, and Shenandoah Counties, Virginia

Ownership Map

Drawing 0.1

OLMSTED CENTER
for Landscape Preservation

National Park Service
Olmsted Center for Landscape Preservation
http://www.nps.gov/oclp/

SOURCES
1. 2002 Aerial Photography Virginia
2. National Park Service

NOTES
Locations and scale of features are approximate. Plan drawn using ArcMap GIS 9.1 and Adobe InDesign 3.0 by Mike Commisso, January 2007.

LEGEND

Railroads
County Lines
Park Boundary
Water
Quarry
Road
Buildings and Structures
National Park Service
Pasture Preserved
Private

0   .375   .75 Miles

Middletown

Norfolk Southern Railway

Shenandoah River

Cedar Creek

Strasburg

Frederick County
Warren County

Frederick County
Shenandoah County

CSX Railroad

55

11

LAND USE HISTORY

PRE-HISTORY TO THE BATTLE OF CEDAR CREEK

Indigenous peoples developing from the nomadic hunters of the 8000 B.C Paleo-Indian Period occupied Virginia's landscape for more than a thousand years before the arrival of Europeans. By the early seventeenth century, English settlements began appearing in Virginia's coastal Tidewater region, the first being Jamestown in 1607. Conflicts with Europeans and introduced diseases, eventually led to the disappearance or relocation of Native Americans in Virginia.[1]

The Virginia government encouraged settlement beyond the reach of the tides after 1690 in an effort to secure land against French encroachment and Native Americans in the mountains west and north. Once considered part of the Virginia backcountry, the first settlements near the study area of this report were located within the northern Shenandoah Valley near the Opequon Creek during the 1730s. Utilizing the sites and travel corridors previously chosen by Native Americans, a mix of ethnic and national groups settled the Valley. English settlers comprised only a fraction of settlement, which was predominately Scots-Irish and German origin.[2]

Historian Warren Hofstra, author of *The Planting of New Virginia-Settlement and Landscape in the Shenandoah Valley*, describes the character of the Scots-Irish and German immigrants:

> They came from diversified small-farm economies in Europe, and they migrated as families. In the New World their desire for a competence in landholding combined with modest means to generate communities of yeoman freeholders who took up and developed middling-sized tracts of land. They created socially and economically integrated settlements with dense networks of kinship, trade, and religious affiliation....This same group had also adopted measures encouraging white servant immigration and restricting the importation of black slaves, assuming that its new population of small farmers would depend on family, not slave, labor on the frontier.[3]

By the late 1730s, westward settlement led to the creation of Frederick and Augusta counties.[4] Shenandoah and Warren counties, originally part of Frederick County, were formed in 1772 and 1836, respectively.

Eventually, relations with North American colonists and the British crown deteriorated, leading to the American Revolution in 1775. The war provoked economic, political, and social change. Although slavery continued to be supported by law in Virginia, the U.S. Congress prohibited the importation of slaves beginning in 1807. This change minimally impacted the Shenandoah Valley as slavery was not as prevalent.[5]

Improvements to the state's transportation networks allowed many Virginia counties and towns to prosper during the late eighteenth and early nineteenth centuries (Figure 1.0). As a result of improved roads, the subsistence farms of the Shenandoah Valley were able to transport cash crops to regional markets. Towns became centers for commerce and the number of gristmills increased. However, the economic stability of the state and Valley region would eventually weaken as Midwestern agricultural in the Ohio River Valley began to thrive.[6]

Throughout the nineteenth century, slavery continued to be at the forefront of controversy eventually leading to civil war. Over 123 battles would be fought on Virginia soil, and the aftermath resulted in landscape devastation. The Shenandoah Valley, considered the breadbasket of the Confederacy, was made into a wasteland.[7]

THE CIVIL WAR AND SHENANDOAH VALLEY LANDSCAPE

In determining the significance of a cultural landscape, characteristics and associated features including, natural systems and features, land use, circulation, topography, vegetation, buildings and structures, and small-scale features are analyzed and evaluated. Commanding officers, prior to battle also analyze the landscape according to similar characteristics, commonly referred to by its modern acronym of KOCOA, which stands for key terrain, observation, cover and concealment, obstacles and avenues of approach:

- Key terrain: Features, such as high ground, which must be controlled in order to achieve military success.
- Obstacles: Features, such as swamps and ravines, which protect the defender and/or impede the attacker;
- Cover and concealment: Areas where elements of an army may be placed without detection or fear of direct or indirect fire, such as woods, buildings and man-made fortifications, even tall grass or crop land;
- Observation: Viewshed areas, such as high ground or buildings providing vantage points for observation of enemy movements;
- Avenues of approach and retreat: Landscape features such as roads, lanes, and areas that allow effective movement of troops during assaults or retreat.[8]

Although not referred to by this twentieth century acronym during the Civil War, these basic principles of analyzing the terrain were used by military officers during the Battle of Cedar Creek.

The natural, man-made and topographic features of the Shenandoah Valley were significant to the outcome of the battle. The rolling topography, including Pout's Hill, Stickley Hill, Hupp's Hill and Three Top Mountain, also referred to as Signal Knob, allowed military leaders to survey and observe the surroundings and plan strategy. The existing road network, including the Valley Turnpike, provided an efficient means of transporting soldiers up and down the Valley. While Cedar Creek and the Shenandoah River formed a natural defensive wall with steep ravines and slopes, the fords and bridges that were originally built for agricultural and residential needs of the communities served as crossing points for both armies. As a result, fords influenced the location of defensive earthworks. The forested areas within the Shenandoah Valley provided an area of concealment, and the presence of open farmlands supported the large number of troops, allowing them to gather for battle. Many of the buildings and structures within the Valley were used as war time housing, headquarters, or field hospitals. Wood fences were occasionally disassembled to build shelters and crude defenses.[9]

The following brief account of the events leading to the Battle of Cedar Creek, the battle itself, and its conclusion, is presented to highlight the role of the landscape in the battle. *Staff Rides: A Self-Guided Tour of the Battle of Cedar Creek*, by Joseph Whitehorne, provides detailed information on troop positions and movements during the battle. It can be found at http://www.army.mil/cmh-pg/books/staff-rides/cedarcreek/ccfm.htm .

The Valley Campaign and Prelude to Battle

In addition to the Shenandoah Valley's natural alignment from southwest to northeast, the Valley Pike road provided a perfect Confederate avenue of approach to Federal positions, as well as a large food supply for southern soldiers. It was imperative for Federal forces to gain control of the Valley.[10]

As early as March 18, 1862, battles were fought in the Shenandoah Valley, with some occurring within the future boundaries of the study area. Under the leadership of Thomas Jonathon "Stonewall" Jackson, and later General Jubal Early, the Confederates dominated the Shenandoah Valley early in the war. However, Confederate power eventually weakened when Union General, Ulysses S. Grant, consolidated Federal forces in the Valley from Maryland, West Virginia, and northern Virginia and placed General Philip H. Sheridan in command. According to Michael Mahon's, *The Shenandoah Valley 1861-1865*, instructions to Sheridan from Grant were as follows:

> In pushing [south] up the Shenandoah Valley…it is desirable that nothing should be left to invite the enemy to return. Take all provisions, forage and stock wanted for the use of your command. Such as cannot be consumed, destroy…If the war is to last another year, we want the Shenandoah Valley to remain a barren waste.[11]

For over a month, small skirmishes would be fought between both armies. However, Early's forces experienced a significant loss at the Third Battle of Winchester on September 19, 1864. Forced to retreat, Early was pushed back as far as Harrisonburg, with Federal forces following in pursuit. Assuming that Early and the Confederate soldiers were no longer a threat, General Sheridan ended his pursuit and withdrew northward, down the Valley, destroying all railroads, canals, mills, homes and crops (Figure 1.1). "The burning," as it was later known, extended as far south as Staunton. Sheridan later reported on the destruction, commenting:

> ...In moving back to this point, the whole country from the Blue Ridge to the North Mountain has been made entirely unattainable for a rebel army. I have destroyed over 2,000 barns filled with wheat and hay and farming implements; over seventy mills filled with flour and wheat; have driven in front of the army over 4,000 head of stock, and have killed and issued...to the troops not less than 3,000 sheep. This destruction embraces the Luray Valley and the Little Fort Valley as well as the Main Valley.[12]

After days of destruction, the Federal army came to rest in positions on the north bank of Cedar Creek on October 10, 1864. On October 13, while on Hupp's Hill, Jubal Early and the Confederate army opened fire on the Federals, causing many Union casualties. After intense fighting, Early pulled back to Fisher's Hill, but continued to utilize Hupp's Hill as an observation point to survey Federal activity near Belle Grove Plantation.[13]

Hupp's Hill and a Signal Station on the top of Massanutten, or Three Top, Mountain provided excellent opportunities for General Early to observe the Union camps and positions situated along Cedar Creek and Belle Grove (Figure 1.3). In preparation for a future attack, Early realized that the majority of Sheridan's troops were stationed along the western edge of the Valley, due to the rough terrain located on the east. Early directed Confederate forces to attack the weak eastern flank of the General's army and raid Belle Grove in order to capture Sheridan who, unbeknownst to them, had left for Washington (Figure 1.4).

On October 18, 1864, General Early formulated a three-pronged attack. The left column, under General Wharton, traveled to Hupp's Hill to wait for attacks that would soon follow east of Cedar Creek. The middle column, under General Kershaw, was sent northeast from Strasburg across Pout's Hill to the Bowman's Mill ford. The right column, under General Gordon, traveled east across the Shenandoah River via the Manassas Railroad bridge south of Strasburg to a small trail on the northern side of the Massanutten Mountain. Gordon's army followed the trail and eventually moved into position at Bowman's and McInturff's fords. Pout's Hill concealed the movement of Confederate forces from Union soldiers.[14]

The Battle of Cedar Creek (Figure 1.5)

At 5:00 am on October 19, 1864, General Early's forces simultaneously attacked the Federal army. The middle column crossed Bowman's Mill ford and attacked the high ground south of the Valley Turnpike and Thoburn's Run containing Union trenches dug into the crest of a ridge facing Bowman's Mill ford, due east of Hupp's Hill (Figures 1.6 and 1.7). Following the attack, they surprised a small Union encampment positioned north of Thoburn's Run, at the crest of another ridge, close to the Valley Pike (Figure 1.8). The locations of the earthwork and encampment, as labeled on Drawing 1.0, were strategically placed to provide points to observe Confederate movement along Harmony Hall ford, Bowman Mill ford, and the Valley Pike (Figure 1.9). However, as these positions were raided by Confederate forces, the steep topography became an obstacle, making it difficult for the Federal soldiers to escape. As a result, there were many Union casualties at the onset of the battle.

As the middle column attacked the Union army positioned near Thoburn's Run, the right column crossed McInturff's and Bowman's fords, approached northward on Long Meadow Lane and attacked a second Union camp, located in an open area east of the Valley Pike, approximately in the same location where Interstate 81 currently crosses over County Route 840.

Advancing from the west, past the Stickley House and Mill to the Cedar Creek Bridge (Figure 1.10), General Early and the left column eventually joined with the two other Confederate forces and surrounded a third Union camp on high ground west of the Valley Pike (Figure 1.11). With assistance from other troops, stationed in multiple areas around Meadow Brook and the Red Hills, the Union army regrouped to defend against Confederate attacks. Bordering the heavily wooded western edge of the large Union camp, an extensive line of earthworks were constructed on high bluffs overlooking possible avenues of approach including, the Valley Pike, Hite Road, Cedar Creek Bridge and Hottle's ford. Along the southern edge, positions were formed without entrenchments, parallel to the Valley Pike. As quoted in *The Guns of Cedar Creek* by Thomas Lewis, the following observation, although not completely accurate as noted in brackets by Clarence Geier, was made by a Confederate officer of the earthworks constructed at the Union encampment:

> The enemy's breastworks were built of strong timbers with earth thrown against them with a deep trench on the inside, being deeper from the bottom of the trench to the top of the works than the height of the soldiers when standing. Thus a step of three or four feet was built for the troops to stand on and fire. The breastworks wound in and out with the creek, some places jutting out almost to the very brink; at others, several hundred yards in the rear, a level piece of bottom land intervening. This ridge and plateau were some fifty feet or more above the level of the creek and gave elegant position for batteries. In front of this breastwork, and from forty to fifty feet in breadth, was an abatis constructed of pine

trees, the needles stripped, the limbs cut and pointed five to ten feet from the trunks. These were packed and stacked side by side on top of each other, being almost impossible for a single man even to pick his way through, and next to impossible for a line of battle to cross over. All along the entire length of the fortifications were built great redoubts or earthworks in the form of squares [none were identified by survey], the earth being of sufficient thickness to turn any of our canon balls, while all around was a ditch from twelve to fifteen feet deep-only one opening in the rear large enough to admit the teams drawing the batteries [this may actually refer to the presence of a series of deep sinkholes lying behind the earthworks near the south end]. Field pieces were posted at each angle, the infantry, when needed, filled the space between...This I believe was one of the most completely fortified positions by nature, as well as by hand, of any line occupied during the war.[15]

Although, earthworks were designed to enhance artillery and military control, the natural slopes and limestone sinkholes found north of the Valley Pike were also used as defensive features.

By 7:30 am, the Confederate forces had driven the Federal forces to positions centered near Belle Grove (Figures 1.12 and 1.13). As the battle ensued, the Federal army deployed into three divisions. Located along the northern edge of Valley Pike, in areas near the Solomon Heater House and Meadow Brook, the first and second divisions held this key terrain for hours before retreating a mile northwest of Middletown (Figures 1.14 and 1.15). The second division, having been forced northward to a partially wooded hillcrest that served as the Middletown cemetery, single handedly fought against the onslaught of Confederate forces, before withdrawing to newly established Union lines beyond Middletown.[16] Theodore Mahr, author of *The Battle of Cedar Creek*, provides the following description of the fighting at Cemetery Hill and supplies an excellent example of how the landscape and its features are critical to warfare:

> Although Getty's plans for hitting the Rebel flank had been frustrated, his retrograde movement to Cemetery Hill proved to be a blessing in disguise. The hill was semi-circular in shape with steep, rugged wooded slopes bordering Meadow Brook on the southeastern side next of Middletown, and a long, coverless approach across marsh ground directly to the south. Curving back to the north, the crest of the hill was covered with thick woods and overlooked the broad, open valley of Middle Marsh Run. At the summit of the hill near the southwestern crest lay the Middletown cemetery. From this location the Federals could command the Valley Pike, which passed through Middletown a half mille to the east. Therein lay the second advantage for Getty now found himself in precisely the right position to form the nucleus of a line of battle facing southwest while at the same time controlling the Pike... As Getty's Yankees assumed their position along the top of the hill, they hurriedly prepared to receive an attack. Some of the troops...began to erect crude breastworks of logs and rails. A portion of the Vermont brigade found the remnants of a low stone wall running along the right of their line and used it to gain some needed protection.[17]

With the return of General Sheridan from Winchester, the morale of the Union soldiers was lifted and the lines were combined and rebuilt. Now facing each other, perpendicular to the Valley Pike, Sheridan and the Federal forces engaged in a counterattack against the Confederate forces of Gordon, Kershaw and Ramseur. With assistance from Custer's Federal cavalry, the Confederate forces weakened and eventually withdrew southward in the direction of Stickley and Hupp's Hills (Figure 1.16).

As it was for the Union soldiers early in the battle, the ravines, marshy grounds, and steep walls of Cedar Creek became barriers and obstacles to the retreating Confederate forces. With the Stickley house now serving as a hospital, the Confederate forces attempted to fight back, but Early eventually lost control as his forces dissolved in an effort to escape the Federal pursuit. Reforming at Fisher's Hill, Jubal Early and the Confederate army retreated southward before dawn the next day, ending Confederate military control of the Shenandoah Valley (Figure 1.17).[18]

SHENANDOAH VALLEY LANDSCAPE FEATURES

Land use

Prior to European settlement, the Shenandoah Valley consisted of forests, thickets, bottomland meadows and clearings caused by natural and cultural factors. As described in early accounts of the Shenandoah Valley, oaks and hickories comprised the majority of the forest and the more fertile soils, and pines and conifers were found scattered throughout in barren sandy soils.[19]

During various stages of forest succession in the Valley, the forest understory, meadows and clearings produced thickets. Based on traveler accounts, thickets consisted of grape vines, ivy, laurel, briars and various perennials. During his exploration across the Blue Ridge near Chester Gap and north along Opequon Creek, John Bartram observed and named beautiful flowers including, Jacea, Gratiola, Dracocephalon, Chrysanthemums, and asters.[20]

While there is uncertainty to their origins, bottomland meadows and clearings found within the Valley may have been created by Native Americans, soil compaction by eastern woodland buffalo, elk and other herd animals attracted to salt springs, periodic flooding, accidental fire or severe storms. An early eighteenth century traveler's account drew a similar conclusion:

> The whole country is a perfect forest, except where the woods are cleared for plantations, and old fields, and where have been formerly Indian towns, and poisoned fields and meadows, where the timber has been burnt down in fire-hunting or otherwise; and about the creeks and rivers are large rank morasses or marshes, and up the country are poor savannahs.[21]

These openings in the forest were of great value to Native Americans and European settlers, who used them to locate dwellings, grow crops and raise livestock. Native Americans typically grew corn, beans and squash, while Scots-Irish and German settlers grew wheat, rye, barley, oats, corn, flax, hemp and tobacco.[22] Wheat and rye, the principal bread grains of the early settlers, were sown in the fall and harvested in the early summer. Corn was grown in the spring for pigs and used for making cornbread and corncakes. Barley, oats, flax, hemp, and tobacco were planted in the spring and harvested in late summer. Barley was used for beer and ale, flax for linen production, and oats were for the horses. Because tobacco functioned as an export and means of currency in the early colonial economy, attempts were made to grow it in the valley as early as 1740. However, tobacco cultivation was not favored within the agrarian cultures of German and Irish immigrants. As a result, it scarcely penetrated the Shenandoah Valley.[23]

Hemp initially provided the motivation for the increasing market development. Military need for cordage created the demand for hemp and the first commercial opportunity for farmers. However, after 1760, with an increase in foreign demand and higher prices to offset the considerable transportation costs, wheat began to carry valley farmers to a new level of surplus production. By 1800, the Shenandoah Valley was the leading wheat producing region in Virginia.[24] Although the emphasis in agricultural production evolved over time from a locally contained agricultural economy to a regionally based market, grain and livestock farming remained an integral component of the landscape throughout the nineteenth century.

Forest land was essential to building and hunting, however many settlers viewed these lands as a hindrance to agriculture. By the end of the 18th century, one-third or more of the forested areas had been cleared for agricultural purposes. In 1796, Isaac Weld observed:

> The neighborhood of Winchester it is so thickly settled, and consequently so much cleared, that wood is now beginning to be thought valuable; the farmers are obliged frequently to send ten or fifteen miles even for their fence rails. It is only, however, in this particular neighborhood that the country is so much improved; in other places there are immense tracts of woodlands still remaining, and in general the hills are all left uncleared.[25]

As settlements grew within the Valley, marshes were drained for agricultural purposes, eventually resulting in natural wet meadows reverting to woodland. As these land uses shifted, the landscape of the Shenandoah Valley remained a mosaic of open and wooded land.

Circulation

Previously used by Native Americans as a migratory route and hunting grounds, the major northeast-southwest route through the Shenandoah Valley, known as the "Great Wagon Road," became a major transportation corridor for European settlers. Because of its importance, many settlements were developed along the former Native American trail (Figure 1.18). On March 3, 1834, the Valley Turnpike Company was incorporated by the Virginia General Assembly, authorizing the construction of a new turnpike from Winchester to Harrisonburg, a distance of sixty-eight miles. The turnpike, funded by private-public investment, was surfaced with crushed stone macadam pavement and eventually merged with a similar road from Harrisonburg to Staunton to comprise the "Valley Pike." Eventually spanning a distance of ninety-three miles, stockholders of the Valley Pike charged tolls for its maintenance (Figure 1.19). During the Civil War, the road was instrumental in transporting artillery and soldiers through the Valley. Evidence of its importance is evident by the great number of battlefields located along its length.

From its beginnings, the Valley Turnpike served as the spine for transportation within the Shenandoah Valley. Eventually, roads would branch out from it to form a network of transportation corridors, connecting settlements with individual farms, industries and crossroads leading to major cities (Figure 1.20).

In Virginia, most railroads built before the Civil War were located east of the Blue Ridge Mountains and designed to connect the Piedmont to the tidewater cities of eastern Virginia. Early railroads built in the Valley included the Baltimore and Ohio Railroad (B&O) connection built in 1834 to Harpers Ferry and the Winchester and Potomac Railroad connection from Winchester to the B&O in Harpers Ferry in 1836. The Manassas Gap Railroad, which figured in the Civil War, was built in 1854. The majority of the Shenandoah Valley remained underserved by railroads until after the Civil War. As the sole authority issuing railroad charters in the state, the Virginia General Assembly was reluctant to have Shenandoah Valley products shipped via the B&O to northern markets. Merchants in Alexandria and Richmond benefited from Shenandoah Valley agriculture and were able to deter construction of a transportation system that would compete with their economic interests. Eastern Virginia continued to be politically dominant, and its elected leaders were able to restrict the expansion of economic outlets for Shenandoah Valley products until after the Civil War.[26]

Building and Settlement Patterns

Prior to early colonial settlement, the Shenandoah Valley had been occupied by various native groups, including the Shawnee, the Susquehannocks, numerous eastern Siouan groups, Catawba's, Cherokees, the various members of the Six Nations, the Delaware, and the Creeks. Used as a central topographic corridor for travel, migration, hunting and planting, Native Americans habitation was apparent throughout the valley from the landscape features found there by European settlers. These features included old fields, mounds, graves and fire-cleared forests. Following Native American precedents, European settlers located their dwellings within open areas near rivers and streams, occupying terraces adjoining the flood plains. In several instances, Europeans located their settlements on abandoned Native American sites.[27]

Typical dwellings built in the Shenandoah Valley by early Scots-Irish and German settlers were rectangular and relatively small log structures with small adjoining fields containing gardens and crops. The bottomlands were cleared for use as meadows and fences were built to protect crops from free ranging livestock.[28] Early fence types were mainly post and rail, but the snake fence which consisted of a zigzag of interlocking wood rails, was commonly used throughout the Shenandoah Valley by the end of the eighteenth century (Figure 1.21). Eventually, log structures were replaced by limestone and wood frame structures.

As commodities were produced, processing occurred simultaneously through the development of milling operations. In 1738, there were at least 34 gristmills within the Shenandoah Valley and by 1775 there were at least 100 mills located on waterways, with the majority found along the Shenandoah River.[29]

Trade and commerce eventually spurred the development of a town and country landscape within the Shenandoah Valley. Unlike tobacco economies, grain economies required specialists involved with processing, storing, or transporting flour. These specialists, along with merchants, clustered in backcountry towns, including Winchester. By 1800, approximately twenty-seven towns would exist within the Shenandoah Valley, creating the distinctive landscape of enclosed farms and market towns (Figure 1.22).[30]

Views and Vistas

During the Civil War, views and vistas were important to military strategy. In preparation of a future attack on Union soldiers, confederate General Clement A. Evans made this observation in a letter to his wife while atop Three Top Mountain:

> What a splendid sight was before me...The vision was limited by the Blue ridge on the right, the Alleghanies on the left and before you it melted far off into a hazy horizon....So elevated is the position that the valley presented the appearance of a vast level plain, the highest hills scarcely undertaking [sic] its surface. The Valley pike, like a white ribbon lay along the center, the country roads looked like foot paths, the woods like parks and the field like little gardens with nice fences dividing....The interest of the scene was of course heightened by the full view presented of the enemy's camp. Nearly every tent was visible. We were able to locate precisely his cavalry, his artillery, his infantry and his wagon train. We could see precisely where he had run his line of entrenchments and where they stopped. Even the house where Sheridan made his headquarters was pointed out. There all was with the roads leading to it, the place where he could be bet [sic] attacked and how the

lines could move, how far to go and what to do, - just like a large map. I believe that we can literly [sic] route them if we attack their left flank. Tonight we will probably move…"[31]

SUMMARY DESCRIPTION OF THE STUDY AREA IN 1864

Based on Gillespie's *Battlefields of Fisher's Hill and Cedar Creek* and Hotchkiss' *The Battle of Belle Grove or Cedar Creek* maps, approximately thirty-eight percent of the study area was forested, with the majority of woodlands found within the southern portion of the study area. The majority of the landscape encompassed by the legislated boundary of the Cedar Creek and Belle Grove National Historical Park was agricultural at the end of 1864, encompassing fifty-eight percent of the total acreage with orchards consisting of approximately three percent.

A network of roads connected residential, industrial and agricultural land uses. The Valley Pike physically divided the landscape into two halves. The road served as the major north-south transportation corridor for early settlers, as well as soldiers during the Civil War. Dispersed along the turnpike, was Belle Grove plantation, the Solomon Heater farm and the Daniel Stickley farm and mill. Middletown appears to the north and Strasburg, with the Manassas Gap Railroad, is located to the south, along the Shenandoah River. Although not within the study area, the Manassas Gap Railroad played a pivotal role during the Civil War by providing an avenue of approach for both Confederate and Union armies (Drawing 1.0).

South of the Valley Pike, roads physically connecting settlements and mills included Long Meadow Lane, Bowman Road and Hite Road. Settlements found in the area included the J.A. Baldwin farm, McInturf farm (Hottle house), Long Meadow, Widow Bowman farm, Harmony Hall, C.I. Hite (Whitham) house and Bowman's Mill.[32] Adjoining these settlement clusters were open areas that produced grains and supported livestock. To the north of the Valley Pike, a network of roads which included, Belle Grove Lane, Hite Road, Old Forge Road, and Miller Lane connected the Miller, Ridenour, and Hottle farmsteads and mills to the surrounding settlements (Drawing 1.0).[33]

The location for historic farmsteads and settlements within the legislated park boundary was directly related to their close proximity to the Shenandoah River and its tributaries, including Cedar Creek and Meadow Brook. Many of the larger dwellings were constructed of limestone, which implies the existence of quarries or natural outcroppings. While documentation has not been found to indicate the local presence of industrial quarries in 1864, small quarry pits have been identified at Belle Grove Plantation (Drawing 1.0).

Small family cemeteries existed on the C.I. Hite (Whitham), Harmony Hall, Long Meadow, and Belle Grove properties. In addition, there were two cemeteries within the study area in 1864. The Middletown cemetery, referred to as Mt. Carmel, was located in the northeast section of the park and occupied key terrain, instrumental in the successful Union counterattack. An unidentified cemetery was located on Belle Grove/Long Meadow Lane. Although both cemeteries were used to bury Civil War soldiers, the unidentified cemetery may have been used solely for this purpose (Drawing 1.0).

Throughout the eighteenth and nineteenth centuries, spectacular views of the Blue Ridge Mountains, Massanutten Mountain, Appalachian and Allegheny Plateaus, Hupps Hill, Pouts Hill, Stony Hill, and Stickley Hill could be obtained from within the boundaries of the study area. During the Civil War, views to and from these areas were critical in providing vantage points for observation of enemy movement.

POST WAR TO THE GREAT DEPRESSION

Having been the scene of so much fighting, there was widespread devastation throughout the Virginia landscape. Although Sheridan's methodical burnings are credited with the destruction of the Shenandoah Valley, the Valley was already experiencing problems by 1862. "The country is almost destitute of every kind of forage or subsistence, for it has been full of armies for a long time," observed Jedediah Hotchkiss, the Confederate army's topographic engineer, while from an encampment at Bunker Hill, 12 miles north of Winchester.[34]

With exception to an increase in wheat production, livestock raising and major field crop production in the Valley decreased between 1860 and 1870 (Figure 1.2)[35]. However, Virginia and the Shenandoah Valley eventually recovered, embracing economic development and technological advances that were revolutionizing everyday life. Although Virginia remained predominately agricultural, increasing numbers of Virginians became employed by others in tobacco factories, coal mines, and textile, flour, and lumber mills.[36]

By the late 1870s, tourism was becoming increasingly important to the state, as well as to the Shenandoah Valley. Due to growing prosperity, wealthy persons built dwellings as seasonal homes. Summer hotels and spas were visited by those seeking fresh air and outdoor recreation. During the early twentieth century, Virginia leaders sought the establishment of a national park to attract tourists. In 1926, Congress accepted the donation of lands acquired by the Commonwealth of Virginia and authorized the establishment of Shenandoah National Park in 1935.[37]

Despite economic growth and technological innovations, the state digressed when confronted with political and social change. During Reconstruction, African Americans made some social and economic progress. However, with the return of sovereignty to local officials after 1876, almost all gains were lost. State laws sanctioned a lower, subservient class and enforced rigid racial segregation.[38]

SHENANDOAH VALLEY LANDSCAPE FEATURES

Land use

Though grain and livestock production recovered, Shenandoah Valley farmers could hardly begin to compete with large farms in the Midwest and the Plains states. With the introduction of the refrigerator car in 1887, distant fruit growing regions were now able to compete in local markets closer to major cities. By the early twentieth century, there was a phenomenal rise in fruit production in the Shenandoah Valley, with apples replacing wheat as the primary cash crop. According to an article taken from the report of the sixteenth annual session of the Virginia State Horticultural Society, *The Outlook for Fruit Growing in Virginia* by S.W. Fletcher, the rush of enthusiasm in apple production often led many individuals to plant in unfavorable locations or in unsuitable soils:

> Large orchards have been planted on soils that have not been proved adapted to apples. Orchards have been planted on low-lying lands where the blossoms will be cut off by frost. In the Valley of Virginia hundreds of acres of apples have been planted on soils that should never be used for anything but farm crops like corn, wheat and grass. I have heard some enthusiastic fruit growers predict that the whole Shenandoah Valley will soon be one vast orchard. I hope not. It is for the best interest of any section that its agriculture be diversified. The heavy clay soils of the Valley, especially those lying low, are naturally better adapted for wheat, corn, and grass, than for fruit. The ridges, with shale and gravel limestone soils, and good air drainage, are excellent for fruit, but poorer for general farm crops. It is wise economy, therefore, to plant fruit only on the ridges and uplands, and to keep the valley lands in farm crops. I hope the time will never come when more than five per cent of the arable land of the Valley is in orchard.[39]

As a result of the increase in apple production, many facilities were developed to support apple production and processing. Other factories included, tanneries, furniture making shops, foundries, hatcheries, textile mills, meat packaging houses, limekilns and bottling establishments.

While fruit production was the most profitable, many farmers had supplementary work that did not compete with the fruit crop. Live stock farming, which included dairying, poultry and hog raising, was the most preferred because of the manure it brought.[40] John Wayland's, *A Bird's Eye View of the Shenandoah Valley*, provides the following observation:

> Within the last decade or two the poultry business of the Shenandoah Valley has reached marvelous proportions. Nearly every farm supplements its income and more than often doubles it with poultry and eggs. Some of the largest poultry and egg shipping houses in the United States are to be found in the Shenandoah Valley. Dairy farming and the breeding of fine cattle, horses, hogs, and sheep have tremendous development in recent years.[41]

In the late nineteenth and early twentieth centuries, the mineral resources of the Valley were increasingly sought after and developed. Mining for iron ore, manganese, brownstone, sandstone, china clay, tin ore, limestone, and shale became an important industry to the Shenandoah Valley, resulting in the development of many industrial quarries. According to Thomas Bruce, author of *Southwest Virginia and Shenandoah Valley*:

> …In days gone by, before the many mineral resources were developed at all, there were charcoal furnaces about…and now new furnaces are being constructed in many places in the Valley to use these deposits of iron ore, and at no place that we know of can limestone for fluxing be gotten so cheaply as in the valley.[42]

Circulation

In 1918, the Valley Turnpike was incorporated into the first state highway system. Designated initially as State Route 3, and later changed to U.S. 11 in 1926, the road remained the regional north-south thoroughfare throughout the mid-twentieth century. Besides its numerous name changes, physical modifications to U.S. 11 occurred throughout twentieth century. Initially an earthen path, the road would eventually be widened and paved with crushed stone and later resurfaced with macadam (Figures 1.23 and 1.24).

During Reconstruction, charters were obtained to build additional railroad lines through the entire length of the valley. This allowed for the formation of two companies, the Valley Railroad and the Shenandoah Valley Railroad. While both were competitors, both companies shared a similar vision, "constructing a railroad system that would assist communities in their recovery from the economic and financial devastation of the Civil War."[43] With limited monetary resources, the two companies sought assistance from outside resources. The B&O Railroad, which leased the Winchester and Strasburg Railroad, sponsored the Valley Railroad and the Pennsylvania Railroad sponsored the Shenandoah Valley Railroad. The B&O and Pennsylvania systems, which were generally oriented in an east-west direction, had begun to expand their systems in the Northeast and Midwest and desired to expand into the South. In 1880, the Shenandoah Valley Railroad was completed from Hagerstown, Maryland to Waynesboro, Virginia. By 1890, the railroad system would fall under the new ownership of Norfolk and Western Railway (N&W). By 1883, the Valley Railroad was completed from Staunton, Virginia to Lexington, Virginia. The Valley railroad was constructed on the west flank of the Massanutten Mountain, while the Shenandoah Valley Railroad was located along the east side (Figure 1.25).[44]

Building and Settlement Patterns

There was a tremendous building boom in Virginia and the Valley during the late nineteenth century. In addition to new construction, older structures were often enlarged and renovated using modern building techniques and styles. New communities were also formed as a consequence of more advanced transportation systems and the development of the automobile.[45]

Views and Vistas

Views available from the mountains and undulating topography were retained throughout the late nineteenth and early twentieth centuries, providing excellent opportunities to capture the sights of the Shenandoah Valley. *The Scenic and Historical Guide to the Shenandoah Valley: A Handbook of Useful Information for Tourists and Students*, by John Wayland, provides an insight on views in 1923:

> At certain places in the Valley, by reason of elevation and outlook, the observer enjoys unusual advantages for extended view. From the hills along Cedar Creek, on the old battlefield, the outlook in every direction is magnificent.[46]

However, by the late 1930s, residential and commercial growth in the valley began to adversely impact the viewsheds within the valley.

SUMMARY: DESCRIPTION OF THE STUDY AREA IN 1937

Based on 1937 aerial photography, thirty-six percent of the study area consisted of forested land. Along the uplands, south of the Valley Turnpike, these areas became fragmented from extensive clearing for agriculture and pasture use. Fields surrounding many previously identified settlements were enlarged and apple orchards and other plantations appeared throughout the study area. Fields encompassed fifty percent of the study area, while thirteen percent consisted of orchards (Drawing 1.1).

The Valley Turnpike became U.S. 11 in 1926 and was realigned and widened in 1929 (Figures 1.26-1.28). As a result of the realignment, the former Cedar Creek Bridge was abandoned and a new bridge was constructed down stream (Figures 1.29 and 1.30). U.S. 11 continued to be the major north-south transportation corridor in 1937. Roads were abandoned south of U.S. 11. The majority of the transportation network was paved and improved (Drawing 1.1).

In 1867, the Winchester to Strasburg railroad line was constructed north of U.S. 11. The rail line eventually became part of the Baltimore and Ohio railroad network. Its location contributed to the establishment of the "Meadow Mills" community and the adjacent limestone quarries. Although early records indicate the presence of small-scale quarries in the early twentieth century (i.e. Conner Lime Kiln), quarry activity didn't begin on an industrial scale until the after the 1930s. By 1937, quarries accounted for ten acres of land outside of the study area boundaries (Drawing 1.1).

Besides the small family cemeteries, Mt. Carmel cemetery remained as the only cemetery within the study area in 1937. Between 1864 and 1937, the cemetery grew larger in size.

The northern portion of the study area experienced more growth by 1937. As Middletown grew, development occurred along U.S. 11 and secondary roads leading to Middletown. Along the southern portion of study area, development was limited to a few isolated areas. While individual properties within the study remained in existence, a majority changed ownership by 1937 (Drawing 1.1).

Although residential and commercial development started to negatively impact viewshed areas in the valley by the late 1930s, uninterrupted views of the Blue

Ridge Mountains, Massanutten Mountain, Appalachian and Allegheny Plateaus and other notable features could still be observed from within the study area in 1937.

THE GREAT DEPRESSION TO THE PRESENT

As a result of World War II, shipbuilding, munitions manufacturing and administrative services, contributed to economic prosperity in Virginia and the Shenandoah Valley in the 1940s. As agricultural production became more mechanized, the retail and service sector industries flourished.

Since the mid-1930s, increased development pressure has dramatically affected the agricultural output of Virginia and the Shenandoah Valley. Tourism continues to provide the economic stimulus to Virginia, generating billions of dollars per year.

Within the civil rights movements, African Americans and women achieved significant victories politically and socially. Eventually, desegregation allowed African Americans greater access to public accommodations, including schools, restaurants, theatres and public transportation. The passage of the Civil Rights Act in 1964, eleven years after the Supreme Court's decision in *Brown v. Board of Education*, began the lengthy process of eliminating discrimination. It was a difficult process. Warren County public schools closed for several years as part of Virginia's Massive Resistance program rather than to integrate, and progress on securing better employment opportunities was almost glacial.

Based on the proliferation of automobiles following the end of World War II, the construction of the interstate highway system and decline of the railroads, the Virginia and Shenandoah Valley landscape has significantly changed. In previous periods, towns and villages were created because of their close proximity to transportation routes and natural resources, and development was compact. However, since the 1950s, large communities continued to develop near highways, but correspondingly elaborate systems of support facilities are established with them. As a result of the sprawl created by these transportation and support facilities, the historic resources and the natural environment in Virginia have become threatened.[47]

SHENANDOAH VALLEY LANDSCAPE FEATURES

Land use

Agricultural production within the Shenandoah Valley started to diminish by the late 1940s. As documented in photographs taken by Marion Post Wolcott in the 1940s, traditional farming practices were still employed and the rural character of the Valley remained evident (Figures 1.31 and 1.32).[48]. While apple production continued as the major cash crop in the 1930s, the cultivation of vineyards and cattle-raising has currently become the predominant agricultural land use.

The increase in suburban developments and limestone mining in the mid-twentieth and early twenty- first centuries has led to detrimental impacts to the

Shenandoah Valley. These impacts which include reduced viewsheds and open space, increased traffic congestion, decreased air quality and water pollution, have resulted in piecemeal losses to the Valley's natural beauty and rural and agricultural character.

Building and Settlement Patterns

As a result of substantial growth and the construction of the Interstate Highway System, the number of people moving to the Shenandoah Valley from the Washington Metropolitan area, Eastern Panhandle and Potomac Highlands of West Virginia and Western Maryland has significantly increased.[49] Unlike traditional neighborhoods surrounding urban centers, development occurring in the Valley is typical of suburban sprawl. These areas are characterized by strip malls, fast food chains and large tracts of land devoted to low density, single family use with large expanses of green space. Isolated from the city, these areas are highly dependent on automobiles.

Growth continues to occur in Middletown and Strasburg. Since the 1930s, population growth has occurred within the study area, specifically along the U.S. 11 corridor and Hite Mill Road areas.

Circulation

The development of a nationwide system of "super" highways was first considered in 1938, but it wasn't until 1956, under the Eisenhower administration, that the system was implemented. The following description from the Virginia Department of Transportation's publication *A History of Roads in Virginia-The Most Convenient Ways*, provides an explanation of the new interstate system that would eventually span over 42,000 miles:

> Construction of this modern road network...involves many problems and radical changes in thought. Under the new program, interstate highways will be insulated from marginal traffic generated by motels, service stations, other types of businesses and dwellings. Traffic entering and leaving these highways will do so at designated points. Cross movements of traffic, with which we are so familiar, will be eliminated...The benefits of controlled-access construction are numerous. A modern, controlled-access road transforms, in many ways, the area through which it passes. Land values increase. This type of road promotes safety, saves travel time, reduces the strain on drivers and aids the economic development of the area. Controlled-access standards also protect the states investment in its highways.[50]

In 1957, the construction of Interstate 81 and ensuing interstates, including Interstate 66, began. Although Interstate 81 was not complete in its entirety in Virginia until 1987, it passed through the entire Shenandoah Valley by 1971.

In 1950, U.S. 11 was further realigned and continued to serve as the major transportation route until the late 1960s (Figure 1.33). Evidence of the frequent realignments of U.S. 11 can be seen in the vicinity of the Stickley complex. In addition to its widening, the sharp curves in the road were straightened to support the increased traffic volumes and speeds (Figures 1.26-1.28). However, as a result of the interstate system, the U.S. 11 subsequently became a secondary transportation route.

In the 1950s as investment was made in interstate trucking, the Baltimore and Ohio Railroad (B&O) faced financial hardship. In 1964, the Chesapeake and Ohio Railroad (C&O) took legal control over the B&O. However, it wasn't until 1987 that the B&O and C&O merged. A few months later the C&O itself was merged into the present CSX railroad system.

Views and Vistas

The views and vistas associated with the Shenandoah Valley are significant as they played a key role in its developmental history and the Civil War. However, within the last ten years, the construction of billboards, retail strip development, excessive quarrying and reforestation have diminished many sites and the significant views associated with them (Figures 1.34 and 1.35).[51]

SUMMARY: DESCRIPTION OF THE EXISTING CONDITIONS

Based on 2002 aerial photography, the study area remains rural in character, however, an increase in the scale of transportation corridors and development has changed the landscape. In 2002, forest lands consisted of approximately forty percent of the study area. Fields occupy fifty-five percent and orchards total approximately two percent of the total acreage of the study area. Although open fields encompass a greater percentage of acreage within the study area since 1937, agricultural production has decreased substantially. As a result, there has been in an increase in forest succession. Apple production, vineyards serving local wineries and raising livestock comprise the major agricultural production within the study area. Since 1937, quarries have grown substantially, consisting of approximately 415 acres (Drawing 1.2).[52]

Located east of U.S. 11, Interstate 81 has become the major transportation corridor and underlying agent of suburbanization within and adjoining the study area. Although new development is more dispersed within the park boundaries, outside of the boundaries, the increased population growth from the expansion of the Baltimore-Washington metropolitan area, has affected the areas near the Town of Strasburg, Middletown and I-81 and U.S. 11 interchange. This development has the potential to adversely affect the historic rural character of the landscape (Drawing 1.2).[53]

With the exception to the development pressures occurring from Strasburg into the lower southeast portion of the study area, the primary growth south of Route 81 are widely scattered and found along Long Meadow Road, and Bowman Mill

Road. Realizing the importance in protecting the natural and cultural resources within Cedar Creek and Belle Grove National Historical Park, preservation efforts by various park partners have initially begun in the southern portion of the park with the acquisition and establishment of conservation easements.

Excellent views can still be obtained from within the study area. However, residential, commercial and industrial development outside the boundaries of the study area, have negatively impacted views to Hupps Hill, Stickley Hill and the Appalachian and Allegheny Plateaus.

ENDNOTES FOR LAND USE HISTORY

[1] *Contact and Conflict the Story of Virginia.* The Virginia Historical Society. 20 Sep 2006. <http://www.vahistorical.org/sva2003/new-southerners.htm>-

[2] Warren R Hofstra, *The Planting of New Virginia: Settlement and landscape in Shenandoah Valley* (Baltimore, MD, The John Hopkins University Press: 2004) 7

[3] Ibid, 82-83.

[4] Becoming Virginians-The Story of Virginia. The Virginia Historical Society. 20 Sep 2006. <http://www.vahistorical.org/sva2003/new-southerners.htm>

[5] Clement Eaton, *History of the Old South* (New York: The Macmillan Company, 1967) 110-111.

[6] Clarence Geier, et al., *An Overview and Assessment of Archaeological Resources and Landscapes within Lands Managed by Cedar Creek and Belle Grove National Historical Park. Volume I: Park History, Previous Research, Cultural Resources and Significant Historic Military and Domestic Themes, Threat to Resource, with Recommendations for Resource Management and Interpretation.* (VA: James Madison University, 2006) p.123

[7] Civil War Sites Advisory Commission, *Civil War Sites Advisory Commission Report on the Nation's Civil War Battlefields* (U.S. Department of the Interior: National Park Service, 1993)

[8] National Park Service, *General Management Plan, Gettysburg National Military Park* (United States Department of the Interior: June 1999) 45-47.

[9] Ibid, p.102-104.

[10] Joseph Whitehorne, *Staff Rides: A Self-Guided Tour of the Battle of Cedar Creek*, Center of Military History, United States Army, http://www.army.mil/cmh-pg/books/staff-rides/cedarcreek/ccfm.htm (1992).

[11] Bruce Catton, *Grant Takes Command: 1863-1865* (MA: Little, Brown and Co., 1968) 342-343; quoted by Michael Mahon, *The Shenandoah Valley 1861-1865: The Destruction of the Granary of the Confederacy* (Stackpole Books, Mechanicsburg, P.A., 2001) 114.

[12] J.E. Norris, ed.,*History of the Lower Shenandoah Valley Counties of Frederick, Berkeley, Jefferson and Clarke*, (Chicago: A. Warner and Co., 1890) 551.

[13] Joseph Whitehorne, *Staff Rides: A Self-Guided Tour of the Battle of Cedar Creek*,

Center of Military History, United States Army, http://www.army.mil/cmh-pg/books/staff-rides/cedarcreek/ccfm.htm (1992).

[14] Clarence Geier and Phoebe Harding, *An Overview and Assessment of Archaeological Resources and Landscapes within the Legislated Cedar Creek-Belle Grove National Historical Park. Volume II: The Cultural Resources Part I: Archaeological Sites and Cultural Features* (James Madison University, Virginia, 2006) p.34

[15] Captain D. Augustus Dickert (1864); quoted by Thomas Lewis, *The Guns of Cedar Creek* (New York: Bantam, Doubleday Dell Publishing Group, 1991), 179-180; Lewis's quote of Dickert appears in Clarence Geier and Phoebe Harding, *An Overview and Assessment of Archaeological Resources and Landscapes within the Legislated Cedar Creek-Belle Grove National Historical Park. Volume II: The Cultural Resources Part I: Archaeological Sites and Cultural Features* (James Madison University, Virginia, 2006) p.157.

[16] Joseph Whitehorne, *Staff Rides: A Self-Guided Tour of the Battle of Cedar Creek*, Center of Military History, United States Army, http://www.army.mil/cmh-pg/books/staff-rides/cedarcreek/ccfm.htm (1992).

[17] Theodore C. Mahr, *The Battle of Cedar Creek*, (Lynchburg, VA:H.E. Howard, 1992) 233.

[18] Joseph Whitehorne, *Staff Rides: A Self-Guided Tour of the Battle of Cedar Creek*, Center of Military History, United States Army, http://www.army.mil/cmh-pg/books/staff-rides/cedarcreek/ccfm.htm (1992).

[19] Warren R Hofstra, *The Planting of New Virginia: Settlement and landscape in Shenandoah Valley*, (Baltimore, MD, The John Hopkins University Press: 2004) p.125

[20] Robert D. Mitchell, *European Settlement and Land-Cover Change: The Shenandoah Valley of Virginia During the 18th Century*, (National Geographic Society, Grant #4381-90, 1993) 37.

[21] Hugh Jones, *The Present State of Virginia*, (Chapel Hill: University of North Carolina Press for the Virginia Historical Society, 1956): 74; quoted in Robert D. Mitchell, *European Settlement and Land-Cover Change: The Shenandoah Valley of Virginia During the 18th Century*, (National Geographic Society, Grant #4381-90, 1993) 26.

[22] 1850 United State Census.

[23] Robert D. Mitchell, *Commercialism and Frontier: Perspectives on the Early Shenandoah Valley*, (Virginia: University of Virginia, 1977) 137-139.

[24] Warren R. Hofstra, " Land Policy and Settlement in the Northern Shenandoah Valley." In Appalachian: Frontiers Settlement, Society and Development in the Pre-Industrial Era, ed. Robert D. Mitchell, (Kentucky: University of Kentucky, 1991) 117.

[25] Isaac Weld, *Travels through the States of North America*, 2 vols. (London: G. Robinson, 1784; New York: Johnson Reprint, 1968), 1:231, quoted in Robert D. Mitchell, *European Settlement and Land-Cover Change: The Shenandoah Valley of*

Virginia During the 18th Century, (National Geographic Society, Grant #4381-90, 1993) 45-46.

[26] Ed, King, "Getting them up the Grade the Norfolk and Western Way", *Trains Magazine,* April 2004, p.67

[27] Warren R Hofstra, *The Planting of New Virginia: Settlement and landscape in Shenandoah Valley,* (The John Hopkins University Press: Baltimore, Maryland, 2004) 20-25.

[28] Ibid, p.38-39.

[29] Robert D. Mitchell, *Commercialism and Frontier: Perspectives on the Early Shenandoah Valley,* (Virginia: University of Virginia, 1977) 145.

[30] Warren R Hofstra, *The Planting of New Virginia: Settlement and landscape in Shenandoah Valley,* (The John Hopkins University Press: Baltimore, Maryland, 2004) 285-288.

[31] Edward Stackpole, Sheridan on the Shenandoah, 2nd Edition (PA: Stackpole Books, 1991) 285-286; quoted in Clarence Geier, et. al., *An Overview and Assessment of Archaeological Resources and Landscapes within Lands Managed by Cedar Creek and Belle Grove National Historical Park. Volume I: Park History, Previous Research, Cultural Resources and Significant Historic Military and Domestic Themes, Threat to Resource, with Recommendations for Resource Management and Interpretation.* (VA: James Madison University, 2006) p.97

[32] Clarence Geier, et. al., *An Overview and Assessment of Archaeological Resources and Landscapes within the Legislated Cedar Creek-Belle Grove National Historical Park. Volume II: The Cultural Resources Part I: Archaeological Sites and Cultural Features* (VA: James Madison University, 2006) p.31-47

[33]Ibid, p. 151 and 316.

[34] Jedediah Hotchkiss, *Jedediah Hotchkiss to Nelson Hotchkiss,* September 28, 1862; quoted in Michael Mahon, *The Shenandoah Valley 1861-1865: The Destruction of the Granary of the Confederacy* (Stackpole Books, Mechanicsburg, P.A., 2001) 70.

[35] U.S. Census Office, *Eighth Census: Agriculture of the United States* (Washington, D.C: 1864) 154-165; U.S Census Office, Ninth Census: Productions of Agriculture (Washington, D.C: 1872) 266-273.

[36] *Becoming New Southerners-The Story of Virginia,* The Virginia Historical Society. 20 Sep 2006. <http://www.vahistorical.org/sva2003/new-southerners.htm>

[37] *History and Culture. Shenandoah National Park* (U.S Department of the Interior: National Park Service)

[38] Ibid

[39] S.W. Fletcher, "The Outlook for Fruit Growing in Virginia," *The Report of the Sixteenth Annual Session of the Virginia State Horticultural Society* (January 10th and 11th, 1912) 12.

[40] Ibid, 7.

[41] John Wayland, *A Bird's Eye View of the Shenandoah Valley,* (Staunton, VA: McClure Company, 1924) 11.

[42] Thomas Bruce, *Southwest Virginia and Shenandoah Valley*,(Richmond: J.L. Hill Publishing Company, 1891) 203.

[43] John R. Hildebrand, Iron *Horses in the Valley: The Valley and Shenandoah Valley Railroads, 1866-1882* (Shippensburg, PA: Burd Street Press, 2001)3-7.

[44]Ibid, 7-13.

[45] *A History of Roads in Virginia-The Most Convenient Ways* (Virginia Department of Transportation, 2006) http://www.vdot.virginia.gov

[46] John Wayland, *Scenic and Historical Guide to the Shenandoah Valley: A Handbook of Useful Information for Tourists and Students* (Dayton, VA: Joseph K. Ruebush Company, 1923).

[47] Shenandoah County, *Shenandoah County Comprehensive Plan* (Woodstock, VA: 2003).

[48] Telephone interview with Patrick Farris. September 26, 2006

[49] Ibid

[50] *A History of Roads in Virginia-The Most Convenient Ways* (Virginia Department of Transportation, 2006) http://www.vdot.virginia.gov

[51]Geier, Clarence and Kimberly Tinkham, *An Overview and Assessment of Archaeological Resources and Landscapes within Lands Managed by Cedar Creek and Belle Grove National Historical Park. Volume III: Cultural and Viewscapes* (Virginia: James Madison University, 2006).p13.

[52] Frederick County, *Frederick County Comprehensive Plan* (Winchester, 2003).

[53] Ibid

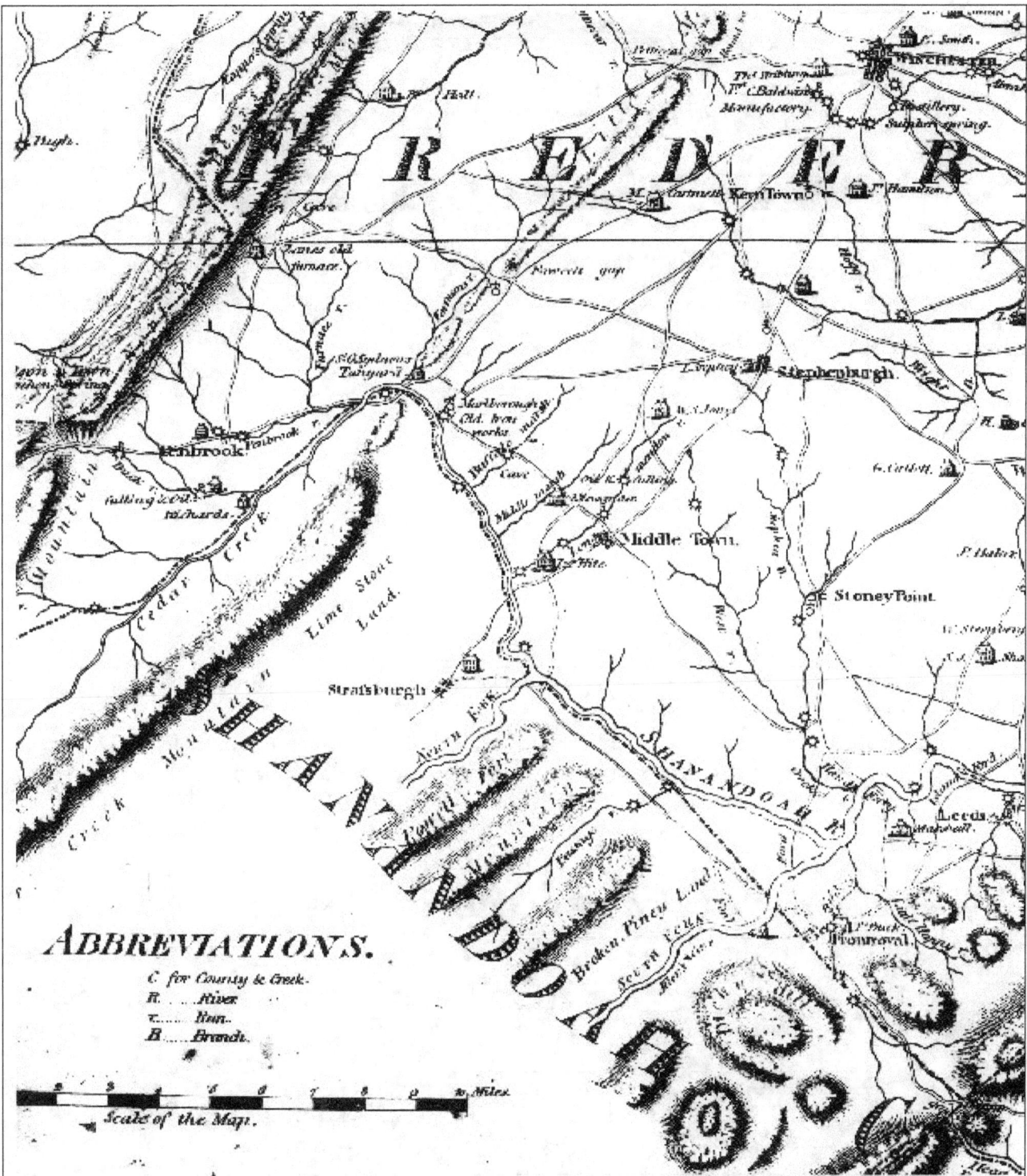

Figure 1.0: A map of the project area in 1809 abstracted from *Frederick, Berkeley and Jefferson Counties in the State of Virginia.* **Notable resources shown on the map include; Strasburg, Middletown, Shenandoah River and tributaries, and Valley Turnpike. Note: "Limestone Land" annotated west of the study area. Source: Handley Regional Library Archives.**

PROPERTY CAPTURED OR DESTROYED DURING THE VALLEY CAMPAIGN OF 1864

Abstracted from Philip Sheridan's Official Report of the Property Captured or Destroyed during the Valley Campaign of 1864.

PROPERTY CAPTURED OR DESTROYED	TOTALS
Horses	3,772
Flour Mills	71
Barns	1,200
Wheat (bushels)	435,802
Corn (bushels)	77,176
Oats (bushels)	20,000
Flour (bushels)	874
Bacon and hams (pounds)	12,000
Hay (tons)	20,397
Fodder (tons)	500
Straw (tons)	450
Beef cattle	10,918
Sheep	12,000
Swine	15,000
Calves	250
Mules	545

Figure 1.1: Philip Sheridan's Official Report of the Property Captured or Destroyed during the Valley Campaign of 1864. Source: Michael Mahon, *The Shenandoah Valley 1861-1865*. (Mechanicsburg, PA: Stackpole Books, 1999).

CHANGES IN LIVESTOCK AND MAJOR FIELD CROPS, VALLEY OF VIRGINIA, 1860-1870

Abstracted from the Eighth and Nine Census

	1860	1870	CHANGE
LIVESTOCK			
Horses	36,566	31,152	-5,414
Milk Cows	28, 709	27,112	-1,597
Other Cattle	62,112	46,964	-15, 148
Swine	147,890	80,468	-67,422
Sheep	71,648	50,336	-21,312
FIELD CROPS			
Bushels of Wheat	1,955, 910	2,148,600	192,690
Bushels of Corn	3,160, 633	1,512,116	-1,648,517
Bushels of Oats	797,526	822,144	24,618
Bushels of Rye	229,174	149,684	-79,490
Bushels of Buckwheat	22,173	3,583	-18,590

Note: Valley of Virginia is defined as the region of western Virginia including the following counties: Frederick, Clarke, Shenandoah, Warren, Page, Rockingham, Augusta, Rockbridge, and Botetourt.

Figure 1.2: Changes in Livestock and Major Field Crops in the Valley of Virginia between 1860 and 1870. Source: Kenneth E. Koons and Warren R. Hofstra, ed., *After the Backcountry: Rural Life in the Great Valley of Virginia 1800-1900* (Knoxville, TN: The University of Tennessee Press, 2000) 9.

Figure 1.3.: View of Massanutten Mountain, looking south from Route 635. Massanutten Mountain provided the Confederate army with views of Union positions and encampments. Source: OCLP, 2006.

Figure 1.4: Photo of Belle Grove Plantation, looking west from the Valley Turnpike (U.S. 11). Belle Grove served as the headquarters of Philip Sheridan during the Battle of Cedar Creek. Source: OCLP, 2006.

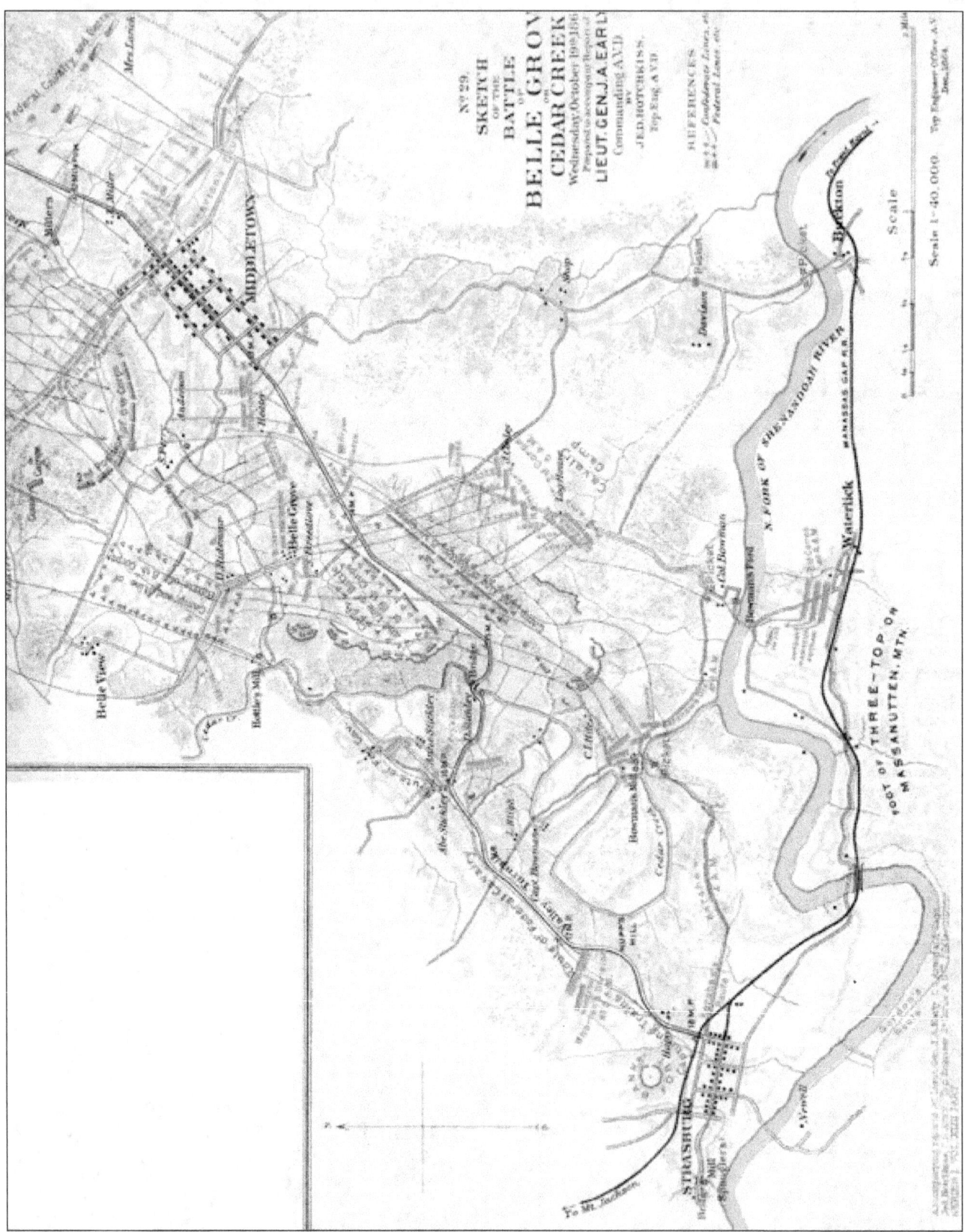

Figure 1.5: Sketch of the Battle of Belle Grove or Cedar Creek, October 19, 1864 by Jed Hotchkiss. Shown on the map are the positions and movements of Confederate and Federal forces during the Battle of Cedar Creek. Source: *The Atlas to Accompany the Official Records of the United States and Confederate Armies: Map 82-9.*

Figure 1.6: Cleared bottomland north of Bowman's Mill Ford, ca. 1885. Note the open fields and the wood board fencing. Source: Clarence Geier, et. al. *An Overview and Assessment of Archaeological Resources and Landscapes within the Legislated Cedar Creek-Belle Grove NHP. Volume II: The Cultural Resources* (James Madison University, Virginia 2006) p.51.

Figure 1.7: Photo of Bowman Mill Ford, looking northwest. Bowman Mill Ford was crossed by Kershaw's Division in the early morning attack on the Federal army. Source: OCLP, 2006.

Figure 1.8: View to the southwest across a large field interpreted as having contained the encampments of Colonel Rutherford Hayes Second Division, VIII Corps. Source: Clarence Geier, 2005.

Figure 1.9: Photo of portion of the VIII Corps earthworks, located on the Whitham property. These earthworks were strategically located as an observation point for troop movement across Harmony Hall Ford. Source:Clarence Geier, 2005.

Figure 1.10: James Taylor sketch of the Valley Pike near the Stickley House and Mill (ruins). Wharton's Division passed this area in route to their attack on the Federal army. Source: James E. Taylor Sketchbook.

Figure 1.11: View of the approximate location of the XIX Corps encampment, situated along the west side of the Valley Pike (U.S. 11). Source: OCLP, 2006.

Figure 1.12: Approximate location where the early mornings skirmishes took place between the XIX, VI and elements of the VIII Corps and Confederate forces. Belle Grove Plantation is in the background. Source: OCLP, 2006.

Figure 1.13: James Taylor pencil sketch of captured Confederate prisoners and equipment in the field to the front of Sheridan's headquarters at Belle Grove (Allen 1983: 159).

Figure 1.14: Photo of the Solomon Heater House, view looking northwest from the Valley Turnpike (U.S.11). During the Battle of Cedar Creek, the house served as a primary cultural landscape feature. Confederate forces moved across the lands east of the house as they moved against Getty's Union troops at Cemetery Hill. Source: OCLP, 2006.

Figure 1.15: Photo of cedar Creek Battlefield, c. 1907. Note the undulating topography and open character of the battlefield. Source: W.E. Huntsberry, NY: A.C. Bosselman and Company, 1907. Handley Library Collection.

Figure 1.16: Photo of Stickley Hill. Besides its importance as the location of Ashby's Battery in 1862, Stickley Hill was used by Colonel Thomas Carter during the retreat of the Confederacy during the Battle of Cedar Creek. Source: OCLP, 2006.

Figure 1.17: Photo of the Stickley Farmstead, looking northeast. The Stickley property was used as a military hospital for Confederate soldiers during the battle of Cedar Creek. Source: OCLP, 2006.

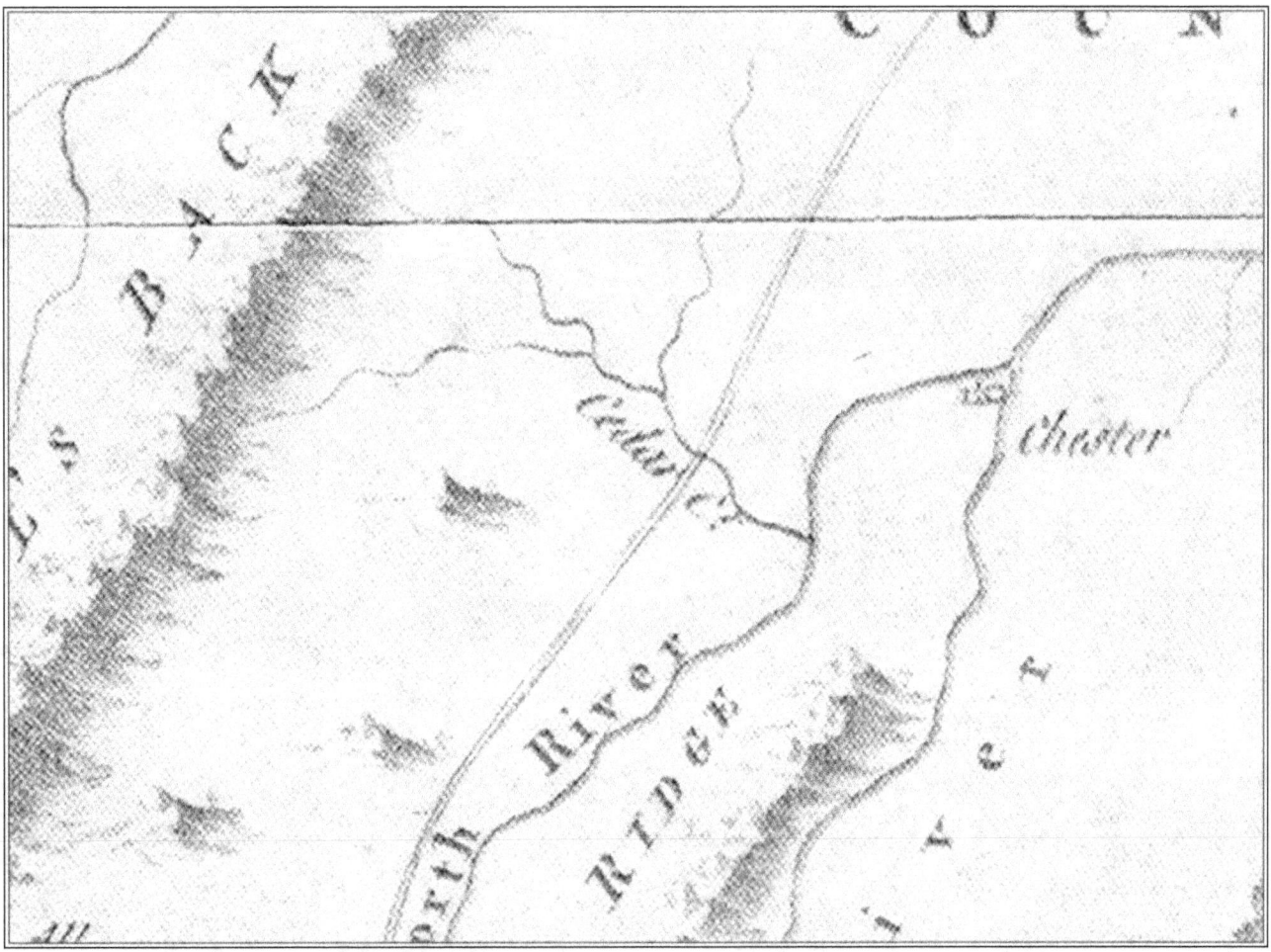

Figure 1.18: Cedar Creek and Belle Grove project area abstracted from *A Map of the Most Inhabited Part of Virginia* prepared by Joshua Fry and Peter Jefferson in 1775. The Great Wagon Road can be seen running through the area. Source: Geier, Clarence R. Phoebe Harding. *An Overview and Assessment of Cultural Resources and Landscapes Within the Legislated Cedar Creek-Belle Grove National Historical Park: Volume II: The Cultural Resources; Part I: Archaeological Sites and Cultural Features.*

Figure 1.19. Photo of a toll house and gate on the Valley Pike, c.1901. Note the proximity of the toll house to the road. Source: Albert Bowen Collection 197-6WFCHS, Handley Library.

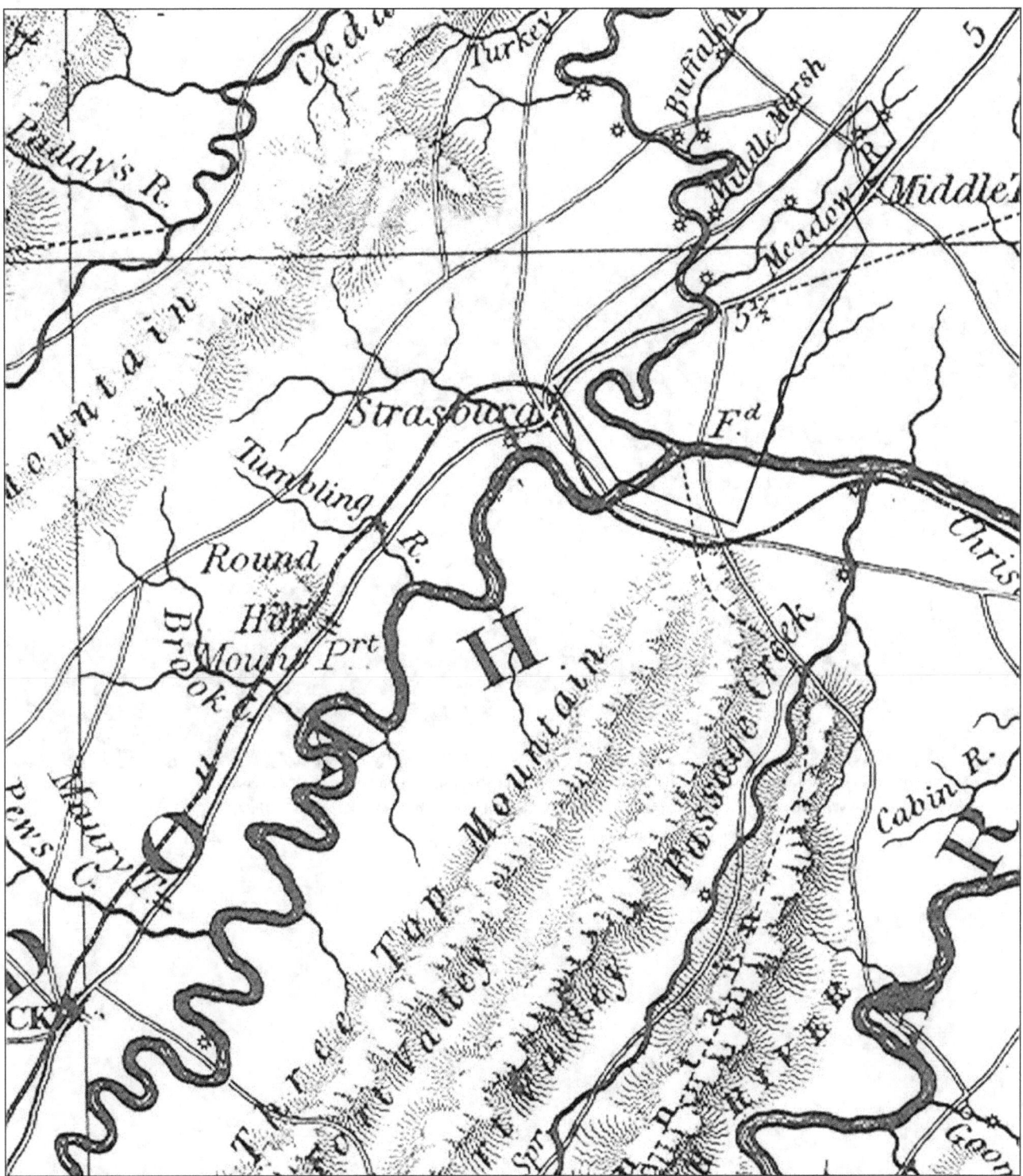

Figure 1.20: Map abstracted from *Map of the State of Virginia* by Herman Boye; prepared 1825, revised 1859. Principal towns, roads, railroads and waterways are shown. Source: Geier, Clarence R. Phoebe Harding. *An Overview and Assessment of Cultural Resources and Landscapes Within the Legislated Cedar Creek-Belle Grove National Historical Park: Volume II: The Cultural Resources; Part I: Archaeological Sites and Cultural Features.*

Figure 1.21: Photo of a snake rail fence commonly used throughout the Shenandoah Valley by the 18th century. Note the open quality of the landscape. Source: William Henry Jackson, *Strasburg, Virginia* (MI: Detroit Publishing Company, c.1892).

Figure 1.22: New towns in the Shenandoah Valley, 1780-1800. Economic growth during the final decades of the eighteenth century produced a wave of town establishments, mostly along the historic Valley Turnpike. Source: Warren R Hofstra, *The Planting of New Virginia: Settlement and landscape in Shenandoah Valley*, (The John Hopkins University Press: Baltimore, Maryland, 2004) 286.

Figure 1.23: Photo of the Valley Pike, taken in 1907, "through Cedar Creek Battlefield, down near the bridge". View toward the SW and Strasburg. Besides the open quality of the landscape, telegraph poles and wire fencing are shown in the photo. The Valley Pike is paved with crushed stone. Source: Handley Library, John Walter Wayland Papers (26.273 WFCHS)

Figure 1.24: Photo of macadamized Valley Pike, taken in 1935, just north of Middletown, looking north. Noticeably different from the Valley Pike in 1907, the road has been resurfaced, widened and lined with stone walls. Near here was the end of Sheridan's ride from Winchester. Source: Handley Library, John Walter Wayland Papers (26.269 WFCHS)

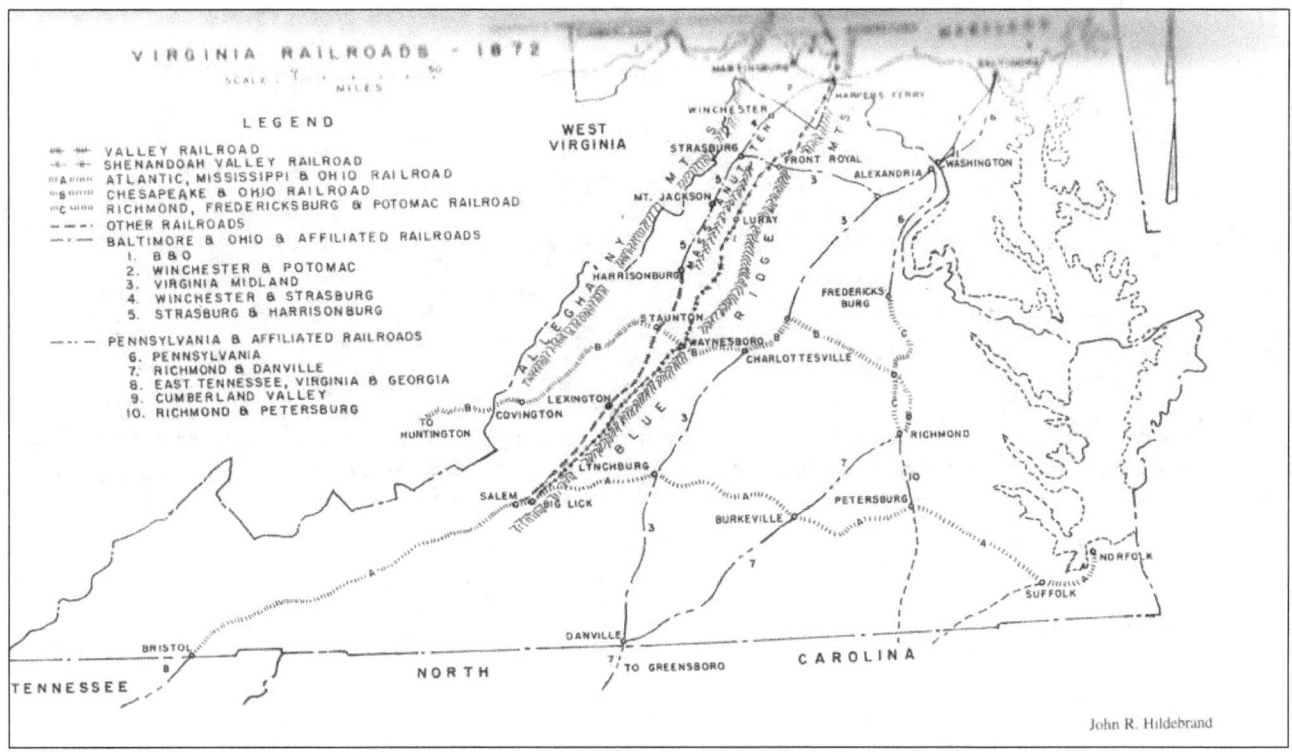

Figure 1.25: Map of the Railroads in the Shenandoah Valley in 1872. Source: Hilderbrand, John. *Iron Horses in the Valley: The Valley and Shenandoah Valley Railroads, 1866-1882.* Shippensburg, PA: Bird Street Press, 2001.

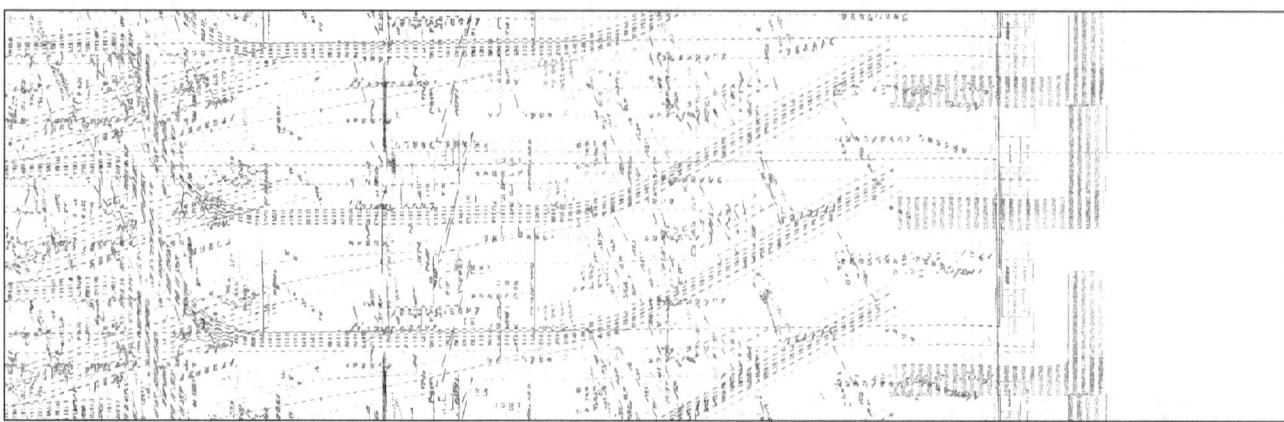

Figure 1.26: Section of a construction document for the realignment and resurfacing of U.S. 11 11 (Valley Turnpike) prior to 1929. The area identified is within the vicinity of the Stickley complex. *Note: Document oriented with north facing up.* Source: Virginia Department of Transportation Plan and Profile of Proposed State Highway Rte. 11 in Frederick, Warren, and Shenandoah Counties (Pre-1929).

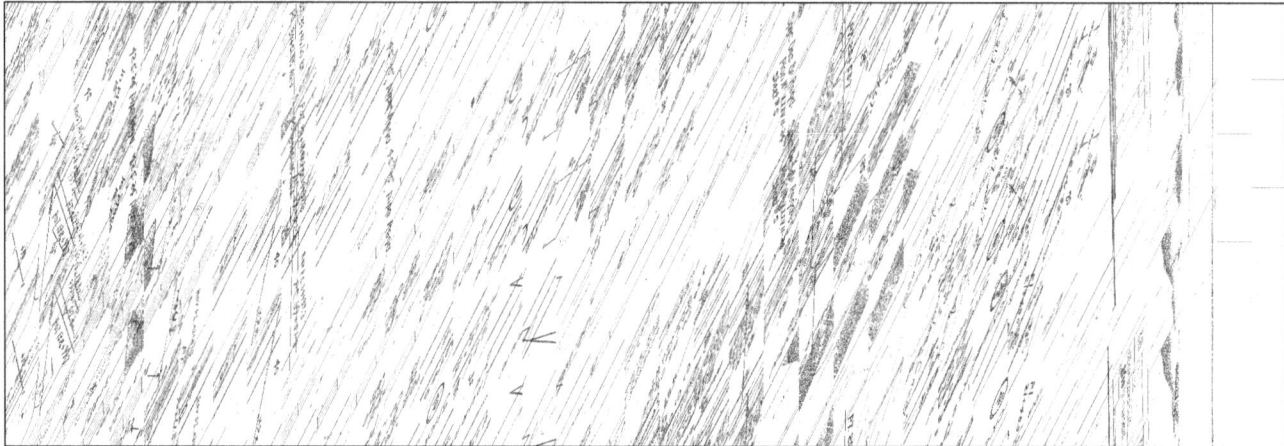

Figure 1.27: Section of a construction document for the realignment of U.S. 11 (Valley Turnpike) in 1929. The area identified is within the vicinity of the Stickley complex. The sharp curve, shown in Figure 1.25, was straightened as a result of the road realignment. In addition, the Cedar Creek Bridge is abandoned. *Note: Document oriented with north facing up.* Source: Virginia Department of Transportation Plan and Profile of Proposed State Highway Rte. 11 in Frederick, Warren, and Shenandoah Counties (1929).

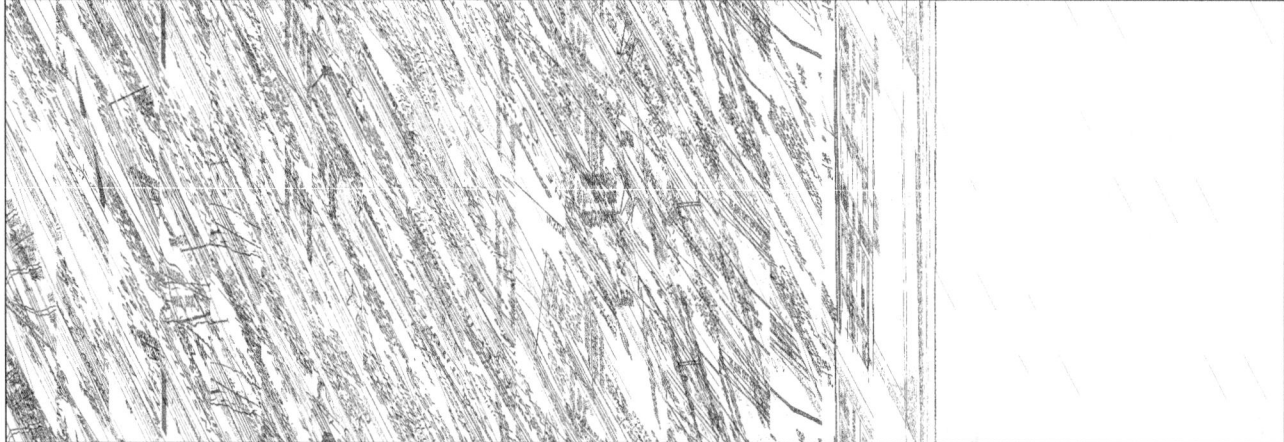

Figure 1.28: Section of a construction document for the realignment of U.S. 11 (Valley Turnpike) in 1950. The area identified is within the vicinity of the Stickley complex. As a result of the increased traffic volumes and inadequacy associated with the 1929 bridge, the divided highway was constructed in 1950. *Note: Document oriented with north facing up.* Source: Virginia Department of Transportation Plan and Profile of Proposed State Highway Rte. 11 in Frederick, Warren, and Shenandoah Counties (1950).

Figure 1.29: Photo of the Cedar Creek bridge, date of photo unknown. The bridge and its connection with the Valley Turnpike played an important role as a major transit route for travelers, merchants, residents and soldiers during the Civil War. Source: Handley Library.

Figure 1.30: With the realignment of the Valley Turnpike (U.S. 11) in 1929, a new bridge (shown above) was constructed. The Cedar Creek bridge, located further upstream to the right, was left abandoned. Source: OCLP, 2006.

Figure 1.31: Photo of the Shenandoah Valley and the apple orchards in blossom, c. 1941. Source: Marion Post Wolcott (Library of Congress, 1941).

Figure 1.32: Photo of a farmer planting corn in the Shenandoah Valley , c. 1941. Note: Traditional farming practices were still utilized in the 1940s. Source: Marion Post Wolcott (Library of Congress, 1941).

Figure 1.33: 1958 aerial photography of the project area showing the realignment of U.S. 11, completed in 1950, and the absence of Interstate 81. Source: USDA FSA Aerial Photography Field Office.

Figure 1.34: View northeast along U.S. 11 showing commercial development (National retail chains and gas stations) in vicinity of Stickley Hill. Billboards, sized to be visible from Interstate Highways, and commercial development are destroying historic views. Source: Clarence Geier, 2005.

Figure 1.35: Photo of the quarries, adjoining the study area. The quarries contribute substantially to the economic vitality of the region and area. However, the quarries have grown substantially, adversely affecting viewsheds from within the study area and giving industrial qualities to the formerly agricultural character of the landscape. Source: OCLP, 2006.

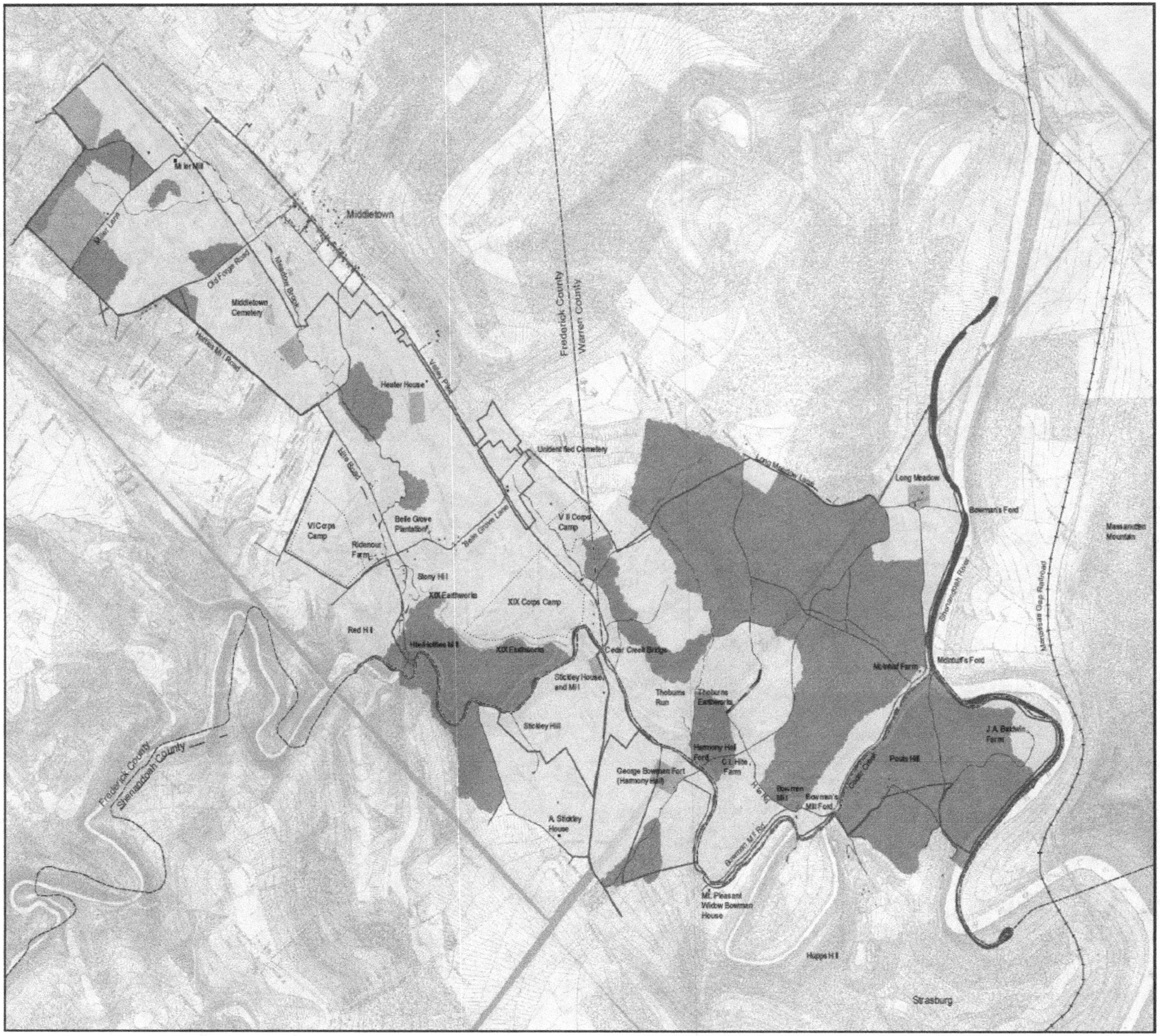

Land Use History Plan

Cedar Creek and Belle Grove National Historical Park

Frederick, Warren, and Shenandoah Counties, Virginia

1864 Period Plan

Drawing 1.0

National Park Service
Olmsted Center for Landscape Preservation
http://www.nps.gov/oclp/

SOURCES

1. Gillespie, Bvt.Lt.Col.G.L. Battlefields of Fisher's Hill and Cedar Creek. In Davis, Kirkley and Perry 1891-1895, Map XCIX. 2. Gillespie produced in 1873.

2. Hotchkiss, Jed. The Battle of Belle Grove or Cedar Creek, October 19th, 1864. In Davis, Kirkley and Perry 1891-1895, Map LXXXII.9, Washington, DC.

NOTES

Locations and scale of features are approximate. Plan drawn using ArcMap GIS 9.1 and Adobe InDesign 3.0 by Mike Commisso, January 2007.

LEGEND

- Railroads
- County Lines
- Park Boundary
- Water
- Road
- Building and Structures
- Cemetery
- Forest
- Field
- Orchard and Plantation

0   .375   .75   Miles

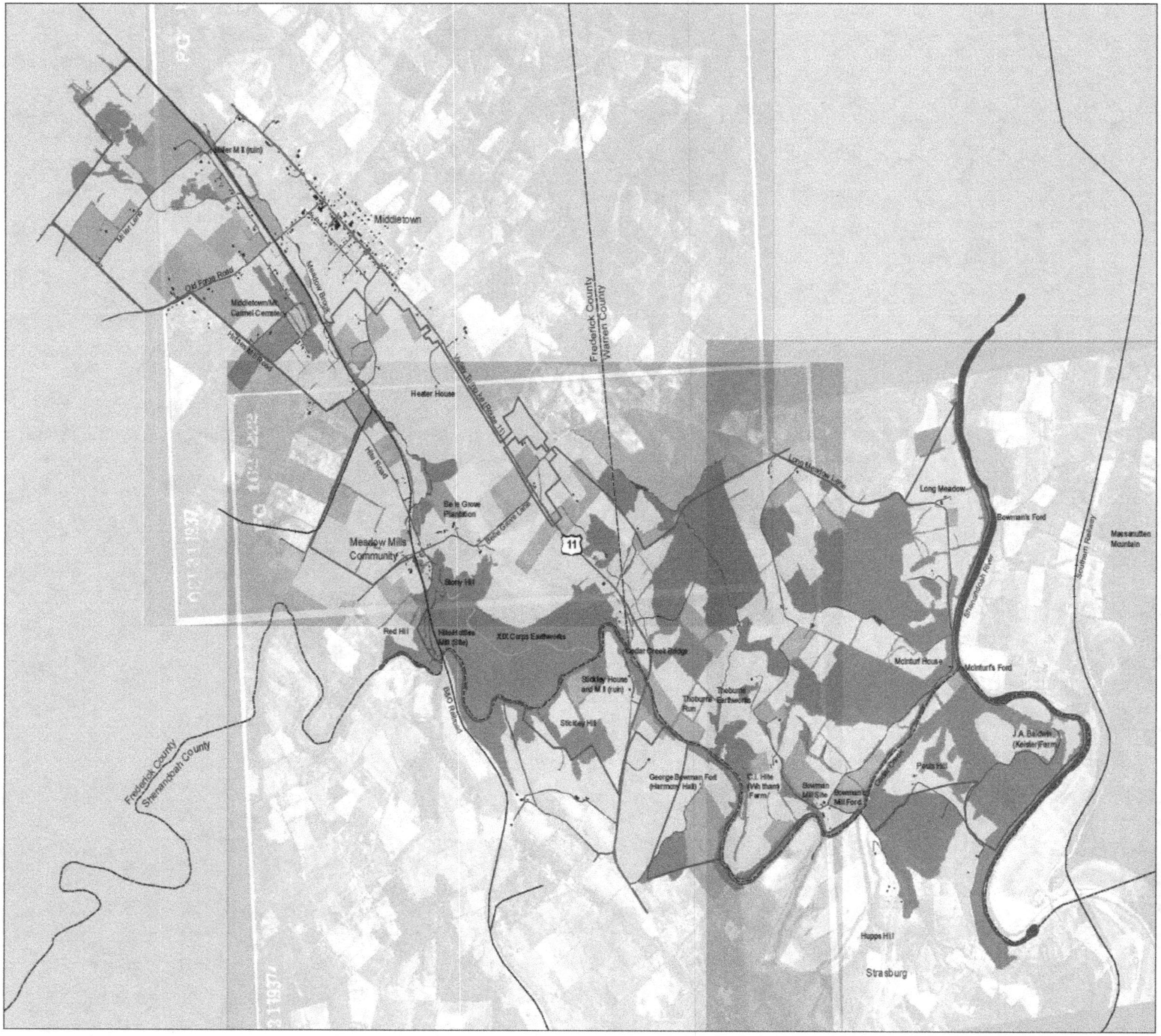

Land Use History Plan

Cedar Creek and Belle
Grove National Historical
Park

Frederick, Warren, and Shenandoah
Counties, Virginia

1937 Period Plan

Drawing 1.1

OLMSTED
CENTER
for LANDSCAPE PRESERVATION

National Park Service
Olmsted Center for Landscape Preservation
http://www.nps.gov/oclp/

SOURCES
1. 1937 Aerial Photography Virginia

NOTES
Locations and scale of features are
approximate. Plan drawn using ArcMap GIS
9.1 and Adobe InDesign 3.0 by Mike Commisso,
January 2007.

LEGEND

----- Railroads
——— County Lines
☐ Park Boundary
■ Water
■ Quarry
■ Road
■ Building and Structures
■ Cemetery
■ Forest
■ Field
■ Orchard and Plantation

0   .375   .75
Miles

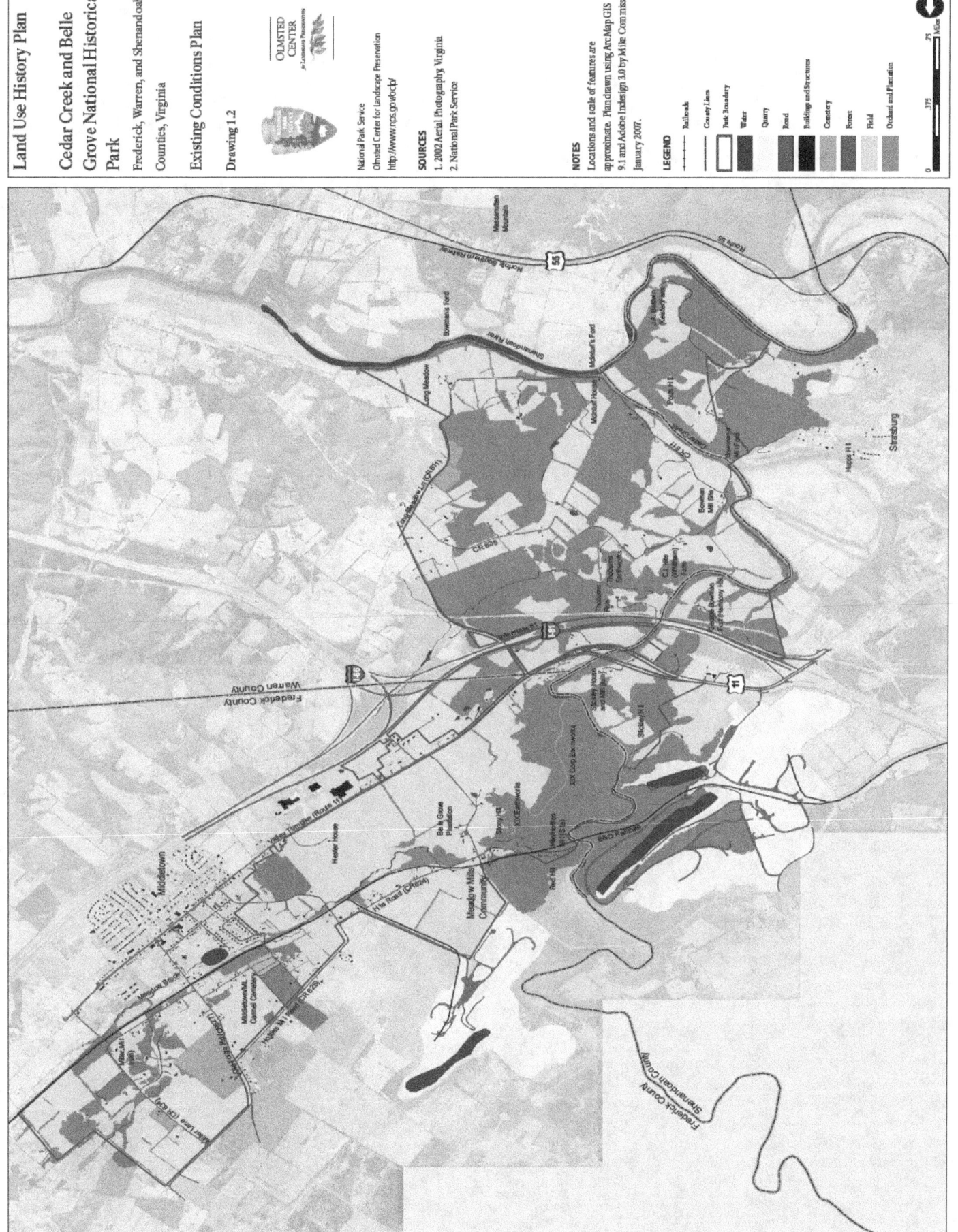

LIST OF REPOSITORIES CONSULTED AND OUTCOMES

FREDERICK COUNTY, VIRGINIA

Belle Grove Plantation, Middletown, VA.
Belle Grove Plantation provides information directly related to the Plantation, including maps, photos, and miscellaneous files. The majority maps and photos that were available at the Plantation were also found at Handley Library.

Frederick County, Winchester, VA.
Has useful website for obtaining a brief history of Frederick County and an electronic version of their Comprehensive Plan. The Planning Department provided up-to-date GIS land use data.

Handley Regional Library, Winchester, VA.
The Stewart Bell Jr. Archives room has many useful information related Winchester and Frederick and Clarke counties. The majority of the information collected for the land use history for Cedar Creek and Belle Grove National Historical Park came from the archival collection at the library. The collection included the John Wayland Papers, maps, photographs, books, reports, and newspaper clippings.

Winchester-Frederick County Historical Society, Winchester, VA
Telephone Inquiry. The Historical Society has no information directly related to Cedar Creek and Belle Grove National Historical Park. Their collections are housed at Handley Library.

SHENANDOAH COUNTY, VIRGINIA

Shenandoah County, Woodstock, Virginia.
Has useful website for obtaining a brief history of Shenandoah County and an electronic version of their Comprehensive Plan. The Planning and Zoning Department provided up-to-date GIS land use data and the Parks and Recreation Department had an electronic version of the Keister Tract Master Plan, completed by EDAW and View Engineering.

Shenandoah County Historical Society, Edinburg, VA.
Telephone inquiry. The Historical Society does not have much information for public access and no information related to Shenandoah Valley and Cedar Creek and Belle Grove National Historical Park.

Strasburg Heritage Association, Strasburg, VA
Telephone inquiry. The Association has no information related to the area of study.

Strasburg Museum, Strasburg, VA
Telephone inquiry. The museum has no information related to Cedar Creek-Belle Grove National Park.

WARREN COUNTY, VIRGINIA

Warren County Heritage Society, Front Royal, VA.
The Heritage Society provides useful information related to Front Royal and Warren County; however had very little information related to Cedar Creek and Belle Grove National Historical Park. Patrick Farris, Executive Director of the Heritage Society, was extremely knowledgeable on all aspects of local and regional history and offered helpful suggestions.

Warren County, Front Royal, VA.
Has useful website for obtaining a brief history of Warren County and an electronic version of their Comprehensive Plan. The Planning Department provided up-to-date GIS land use data.

OTHER

Boston Public Library- Copley Branch, Boston, Massachusetts.
Has most published sources on the State of Virginia, but limited unique information on the Shenandoah Valley.

Carrier Library-James Madison University, Harrisonburg, VA.
The special collections have many invaluable materials related to the Shenandoah Valley, specifically the report, *European Settlement and Land-Cover Change: The Shenandoah Valley of Virginia During the 18th Century* by Robert Mitchell, Edward Connor, and Warren Hofstra.

BIBLIOGRAPHY

BOOKS AND PUBLISHED SOURCES

Bruce, Thomas. *Southwest Virginia and Shenandoah Valley*. Richmond: J.L. Hill
 Publishing Company, 1891.

Civil War Sites Advisory Commission. *Civil War Sites Advisory Commission
 Report on the Nation's Civil War Battlefield*. U.S. Department of the
 Interior: National Park Service, 1993.

Clement, Eaton. *History of the Old South*. New York: The MacMillan
 Company, 1967.

Hildebrand, John R. *Iron Horses in the Valley: The Valley and Shenandoah
 Valley Railroads, 1866-1882*. Shippensburg, PA: Burd Street Press,
 2001.

Hofstra, Warren R. "Land Policy and Settlement in the Northern Shenandoah
 Valley." In Appalachian: Frontiers Settlement, Society and Development
 in the Pre-Industrial Era, ed. Robert D. Mitchell. Kentucky: University
 of Kentucky, 1991.

Hofstra, Warren R. *The Planting of New Virginia: Settlement and Landscape in
 the Shenandoah Valley*. Baltimore, MD: The John Hopkins University
 Press, 2004.

Hunt, Charles B. *Natural Regions of the United States and Canada*. San Francisco,
 CA: W. H. Freeman and Company, 1967.

Kercheval, Samuel. *A History of the Valley of Virginia*. Strasburg, VA:
 Shenandoah Publishing House, 1925.

King, Ed. "Getting them up the Grade the Norfolk and Western Way," *Trains
 Magazine*. April 2004.

Koons, Kenneth E. and Warren R. Hofstra, ed. *After the Backcountry: Rural Life
 in the Great Valley of Virginia 1800-1900*. Knoxville, TN: The University
 of Tennessee Press. 2000.

Kuennecke, Berd. *An Atlas of Virginia: 17th, 18th and Early 19th Centuries*.
 Dubuque, Iowa: Kendell/Hunt, 1989.

Mahon, Michael. *The Shenandoah Valley 1861-1865*. Mechanicsburg, P.A: Stackpole Books, 1999.

Mahr, Theodore C. *The Battle of Cedar Creek*. Lynchburg, VA: H.E. Howard, 1992.

Mitchell, Robert D. *Commercialism and Frontier: Perspectives on the Early Shenandoah Valley*. Virginia: The University of Virginia, 1977.

National Park Service. *General Management Plan, Gettysburg National Military Park*. Washington, D.C: U.S. Department of the Interior, 1999.

Norris, J. E, ed. *History of the Lower Shenandoah Valley Counties of Frederick, Berkeley, Jefferson and Clarke*. Chicago: A. Warner and Co., 1890.

Nowak, Lisa and Eliot Foulds. *Cultural Landscape for Booker T. Washington National Monument*. Boston, MA: Olmsted Center for Landscape Preservation-National Park Service, 14.

Wayland, John. *Scenic and Historical Guide to the Shenandoah Valley: A Handbook of Useful Information for Tourists and Students*. Dayton, Virginia: Joseph K. Ruebush Company, 1923.

Wayland, John. *A Bird's Eye View of the Shenandoah Valley*. Staunton, VA: McClure Company, 1924.

REPORTS AND UNPUBLISHED MATERIALS

EDAW and View Engineering. *Keister Tract Master Plan*. Prepared for Shenandoah County Parks and Recreation, 2005.

Fletcher, S.W. "The Outlook for Fruit Growing in Virginia." *The Report of the Sixteenth Annual Session of the Virginia State Horticultural Society*. (1912): 6-12.

Geier, Clarence R., and Phoebe Harding. *An Overview and Assessment of Cultural Resources and Landscapes within the Legislated Cedar Creek-Belle Grove NHP: Volume II: The Cultural Resources. Part I: Archeological Sites and Cultural Features*. Department of Sociology and Anthropology, James Madison University, Harrisonburg, VA, 2006.

Geier, Clarence R., and Phoebe Harding. (Draft) *An Overview and Assessment of Cultural Resources and Landscapes within the Legislated Cedar*

Creek-Belle Grove NHP: Volume I. Department of Sociology and Anthropology, James Madison University, Harrisonburg, VA, 2006.

Mitchell, Robert D., et al. *European Settlement and Land-Cover Change: The Shenandoah Valley of Virginia during the 18th Century.* National Geographic Society Grant #4381-90 (1991-1992), June 1993.

Oudemool, Lisa, et al. *Cultural Landscape Report: Saratoga Battlefield-Volume 1: Site History, Existing Conditions, and Analysis.* National Park Service, Olmsted Center for Landscape Preservation, Boston, Massachusetts, 2002.

MAPS, PLANS, AND DRAWINGS

Boye, Herman. *Map of the State of Virginia* prepared in 1825 and revised in 1859 by L.v. Buchholtz.

Davis, Maj. George B., Leslie J. Perry and Joseph Kirkley. *Atlas to Accompany the Official Records of the Union and Confederate Armies.* Washington, DC: Government Printing Office, 1891-1895.

Gillespie, Bvt. Lt. Col. G. L. *Map of the Battlefield of Cedar Creek, Va. Fought on Oct. 19th, 1864 and the Cavalry Fight of Tom's Brook fought on Oct. 9, 1864. Bvt. Lt. Col. G. L. Gillespie:* Map LXIX.3. 1866.

Gillespie, Bvt. Lt. Col. G. L. *The Battle of Belle Grove or Cedar Creek, Oct. 19, 1864.* Map LXXXII.1864

Fry, Joshua and Peter Jefferson. *A Map of the Most Inhabited Part of Virginia.* 1776.

Hotchkiss, Jed. *Pencil sketch for The Battle of Belle Grove or Cedar Creek, Oct. 19, 1864.* http://memory.loc.gov/ammem/collections/maps/hotchkiss/

Hotchkiss, Jed. *The Battle of Belle Grove or Cedar Creek, Oct. 19, 1864.* http://memory.loc.gov/ammem/collections/maps/hotchkiss/

Jackson, William Henry. *Strasburg, Shenandoah Valley.* Detroit Publishing Company, DET 4a32833. c. 1892.

Lake, D. J. & Co. *An Atlas of Shenandoah and Page Counties, Virginia.* F. Bourquin, Philadelphia, Pa (reprinted by Samuel, Irene and Samuel, Jr. Koontz, Good Printers, Harrisonburg, VA) 1885.

Lathrop, J. M. and A. W. Dayton. *An Atlas of Frederick County, Virginia*. Lake & Co., Philadelphia, Pa (reprinted in 1997 by GP Hammond Publishing Co., Strasburg, VA).

Taylor, James E. *Sketchbook: With Sheridan Up the Valley in 1864*. The Western Reserve Historical Society, Cleveland, OH.1864.

Virginia Department of Transportation. *Plan and Profile of Proposed State Highway Rte. 33 in Shenandoah County*. 1930.

Virginia Department of Transportation. *Plan and Profile of Proposed State Highway Rte. 33 in Frederick, Warren, and Shenandoah County*. 1929.

Virginia Department of Transportation. *Plan and Profile of Proposed State Highway Rte. 33 in Frederick County*. 1931.

Virginia Department of Transportation. *Plan and Profile of Proposed State Highway Rte. 11 in Shenandoah County*. 1935.

Virginia Department of Transportation. *Plan and Profile of Proposed State Highway Rte. 11 in Frederick, Warren and Shenandoah County*. 1950.

Virginia Department of Transportation. *Plan and Profile of Proposed State Highway Rte. 11 in Shenandoah County*. 1967.

Virginia Department of Transportation. *Plan and Profile of Proposed State Highway Rte. 11 in Frederick County*. 1955.

Virginia Department of Transportation. *Plan and Profile of Proposed State Highway Rte. 81 in Shenandoah County*. 1965.

Virginia Department of Transportation. *Plan and Profile of Proposed State Highway Rte. 81 in Frederick County*. 1965.

Wolcott, Marion Post. *Planting corn in the Fertile Farmlands of the Valley*. Library of Congress, #8cl2066. 1941.

Wolcott, Marion Post. *Apple Orchards in Blossom in the spring in the Fertile Shenandoah Valley*. Library of Congress, #2000038076. 1941.

WEB SOURCES

Maptech. Historic USGS topographic maps. 2006.
  http://www.historical.maptech.com/

Library of Congress American Memory. *The Hotchkiss Map Collection.* 13 April
  2007. http://memory.loc.gov/ammem/index.html

The Virginia Historical Society. *Contact and Conflict the Story of Virginia.* 20
  Sept 2006. http://www.vahistorical.org/sva2003/new-southerners.htm.

Thomas III, William G. "The Chesapeake Bay," *Southern Spaces.* 2004.
  http://southernspaces.org/contents/2004/thomas/2b.htm.

Virginia Department of Transportation. *A History of Roads in Virginia-The Most
  Convenient Ways.* 2006. <http://www.vdot.virginia.gov>

Whitehorne, Joseph W.A. *Staff Rides: A Self-Guided Tour of the Battle of Cedar
  Creek.* Center of Military History, United States Army. 1992.
  http://www.army.mil/cmh-pg/books/staff-rides/cedarcreek/ccfm.htm.

www.ingramcontent.com/pod-product-compliance
Lightning Source LLC
Chambersburg PA
CBHW081429310526
45790CB00020B/2230